What Kind of God?

MISSIONAL WISDOM LIBRARY
RESOURCES FOR CHRISTIAN COMMUNITY

The Missional Wisdom Foundation experiments with and teaches about alternative forms of Christian community. The definition of what constitutes a Christian community is shifting as many seek spiritual growth outside of the traditional confines of church. Christians are experimenting with forming communities around gardens, recreational activities, coworking spaces, and hundreds of other focal points, connecting with their neighbors while being aware of the presence of God in their midst. The Missional Wisdom Library series includes resources that address these kinds of communities and their cultural, theological, and organizational implications.

Series Editor: Larry Duggins

>   vol. 1: *Missional. Monastic. Mainline.: A Guide to Starting Missional Micro-Communities in Historically Mainline Traditions*, by Elaine A. Heath and Larry Duggins

>   vol. 2: *Simple Harmony: Thoughts on Holistic Christian Life*, by Larry Duggins and Elaine A. Heath

>   vol. 3: *Together: Community as a Means of Grace*, by Larry Duggins

>   vol. 5: *Credulous: A Journey through Life, Faith, and the Bulletin*, by Andrea L. Lingle

FORTHCOMING TITLES:

>   *The Julian Way: Towards a Theology of Fulness for All of God's People*, by Justin Hancock

>   *Virtuous Friendship: The New Testament, Grego-Roman Friendship Language, and Contemporary Community*, by Douglas A. Hume

What Kind of God?

Reading the Bible with a Missional Church

Bret Wells

With contributions from
Larry Duggins, Heidi A. Miller, and Denise Crane
Foreword by Elaine A. Heath

CASCADE Books • Eugene, Oregon

WHAT KIND OF GOD?
Reading the Bible with a Missional Church

Missional Wisdom Library: Resources for Christian Community 4

Copyright © 2018 Bret Wells. All rights reserved. Except for brief quotations in critical publications or reviews, no part of this book may be reproduced in any manner without prior written permission from the publisher. Write: Permissions, Wipf and Stock Publishers, 199 W. 8th Ave., Suite 3, Eugene, OR 97401.

Cascade Books
An Imprint of Wipf and Stock Publishers
199 W. 8th Ave., Suite 3
Eugene, OR 97401

www.wipfandstock.com

PAPERBACK ISBN: 978-1-5326-1471-2
HARDCOVER ISBN: 978-1-5326-1473-6
EBOOK ISBN: 978-1-5326-1472-9

Cataloguing-in-Publication data:

Names: Wells, Bret, author. | Duggins, Larry, contributor. | Miller, Heidi A., contributor. | Crane, Denise, contributor. | Heath, Elaine A., foreowrd.

Title: What kind of God? : reading the bible with a missional church / by Bret Wells ; with contributions from Larry Duggins, Heidi A., Millier, and Denise Crane ; foreword by Elaine A. Heath.

Description: Eugene, OR : Cascade Books, 2018 | Missional Wisdom Library: Resources for Christian Community 4 | Includes bibliographical references.

Identifiers: ISBN 978-1-5326-1471-2 (paperback) | ISBN 978-1-5326-1473-6 (hardcover) | ISBN 978-1-5326-1472-9 (ebook)

Subjects: LCSH: Missions—Biblical teaching. | Missions—Theory—Biblical teaching.

Classification: BV2073 .W43 2018 (print) | BV2073 .W43 (ebook)

Manufactured in the U.S.A. APRIL 3, 2018

Scripture quotations marked (NIV) are taken from the Holy Bible, New International Version®, NIV®. Copyright © 1973, 1978, 1984, 2011 by Biblica, Inc.™ Used by permission of Zondervan. All rights reserved worldwide. www.zondervan.com. The "NIV" and "New International Version" are trademarks registered in the United States Patent and Trademark Office by Biblica, Inc.™

Scripture quotations marked (NRSV) are taken from the New Revised Standard Version Bible, copyright 1989, Division of Christian Education of the National Council of the Churches of Christ in the United States of America. Used by permission. All rights reserved.

For Rachel, who baffles me with her willingness to read words she's already listened to and read a million times . . . and for having been willing to listen and read a million times in the first place.

Author

Bret Wells, Leader and Managing Director of the Missional Wisdom Foundation, Leadership Coach (PCC), and Minister with The Gathering in Burleson, Texas.

Additional Contributors

Denise Crane, Leader and Managing Director of the Missional Wisdom Foundation.

Larry Duggins, Executive Director and Cofounder of the Missional Wisdom Foundation.

Heidi A. Miller, Leader and Managing Director of the Missional Wisdom Foundation, Assistant Professor of Christian Worship at Perkins School of Theology, Southern Methodist University.

Contents

Abbreviations | ix
Foreword: What Kind of God Is God? —Elaine A. Heath | xi
Preface | xvii

1. What Does It All Mean? | 1
2. Genesis 1–2: The Community of Love | 24
3. Who Are We? | 44
4. Isaiah 56–59: Who Will We Become? | 56

INTERLUDES ON JESUS

Jesus and the Bleeding Woman:
    Transforming the Community Story —Heidi A. Miller | 79
John 4: "I Am" Sent Her —Larry Duggins | 97
Philippians 2: To Want and to Do —Larry Duggins | 105

5. Philippians 4:4–9: Think about Such Things | 113
6. Revelation 21:1—22:5: Now Among the People | 127
7. Little Children and One Fat Ox | 143

Bibliography | 155

Abbreviations

AD	Anno Domini
AMW	Academy for Missional Wisdom
BCE	Before Common Era
COO	Chief Operating Officer
1 Cor	First Corinthians
CSS	Cascading Style Sheets
Deut	Deuteronomy
ed.	editor
eds.	editors
ELCA	Evangelical Lutheran Church in America
et al.	et alia
Exod	Exodus
FBI	Federal Bureau of Investigation
Gen	Genesis
GPS	Global Positioning System
Isa	Isaiah
IVP	InterVarsity Press
Lev	Leviticus
MWF	Missional Wisdom Foundation
NIV	New International Version
NRSV	New Revised Standard Version
Numb	Numbers
Phil	Philippians
Ps	Psalm
Rev	Revelation

Abbreviations

Rev.	Reverend
RV	recreational vehicle
1 Sam	First Samuel
2 Sam	Second Samuel
SMU	Southern Methodist University
SoCe	South Central (neighborhood of Wichita, Kansas)
UMC	United Methodist Church
WYSIWYG	What You See Is What You Get

Foreword

What Kind of God Is God?

Elaine A. Heath

WE WERE GATHERED IN a smallish, stuffy classroom, sunlight filtering through dusty windows. Outside, Pittsburgh bustled in its perpetual cacophony of traffic, sirens, and jackhammers. This was the Introduction to the Bible class for undergraduates at Duquesne University. I was a PhD student in my last semester before comps and the dissertation, and teaching this class was part of my preparation for a vocation as a professor. The biggest challenge was addressing the multiple responsible methods of interpretation of Scripture. I wanted students to know that there are several ways to approach the text, but I didn't want to confuse them.

Looking out across the thirty or so young adults I wondered what they would make of today's topic, the Sermon on the Mount. Most of the students had grown up in church but few of them—Catholic or mainline Protestant—were seemingly familiar with the Bible.

We had made it through the Old Testament with more than a little controversy. Do the two creation stories in Genesis contradict each other? What kind of God would command *'cherem*, the annihilation of an entire village of people? Why is Jephthah considered a hero in Hebrews for murdering his innocent daughter in Judges? What is a traditional marriage, really, when you have heroes like Jacob marrying two sisters and owning concubines, or David with multiple wives and concubines—and what's the deal with Levirate marriage?[1] Did God will all of that or did it just happen? Was Jonah an historic figure or the lead character in a satire?

We had also made it through the deuterocanonical texts—the books of the Bible that are not in the Protestant canon. More than a few students were stunned to realize that there are different canons of Scripture depending upon one's Christian tradition. Is it possible to reconcile the doctrine of the inspiration of Scripture with multiple canons? What about inerrancy and infallibility? There was also the matter of Jesus being a Jew and the Hebrew Bible being the only Bible of Jesus and the apostles. All this Jewishness was a surprise to most of the Christians.

Now we were into the gospels. What new disturbance would find us today?

"Hello, everyone," I said cheerily. "Today we are talking about the Sermon on the Mount. I trust that all of you made it through Matthew 5–7. But let's not start with content, authorship, or any of that. Let's begin with the raw experience of the text. What did you *feel* when you read the Sermon on the Mount? What did you *wonder*?" Silence. A few people stared at the floor, usually a dead giveaway that they hadn't done their homework. A student who normally kept quiet thrust her hand into the air. She looked upset. Urgent.

"Yes, Sarah?" I asked.[2]

"I can't *believe* this!" she shouted, jolting the drowsy football player to attention. "Yahweh[3] was bad enough, but Jesus is impossible!! No one can live this way. He's telling you to turn the other cheek, forgive people when they do terrible things to you. What the hell?!"

---

1. Levirate marriage was the ancient middle-eastern practice of a widow's brother-in-law being required to marry her to continue the dead brother's family line. In the story of Ruth, Boaz must tend to Levirate requirements before he can marry Ruth.

2. I have changed the student's name for the sake of privacy.

3. Yahweh is the transliteration of the Hebrew name for God that was translated "Jehovah" in the King James translation of the Bible. In Hebrew this name is YHWH, meaning "I Am."

Foreword

What indeed?

Sarah's visceral encounter with the gospel is one that most church people never have because of domesticated readings of Scripture that have shaped their Christian formation. Sarah had been used to thinking of Jesus the way most five-year-olds do—baby Jesus meek and mild, or nice Jesus with the baby sheep. Coming face to face with the shocking rigor of Jesus' commands and her own inability to follow them infuriated her, just as it did so many of Jesus' contemporaries.

Every student leaned forward, listening, and we dove into the central question of the Bible: What kind of God is God? If, as the Apostle Paul claims in Colossians 1:15, Jesus is the exact image of the unseen God, then what is that God like? And how might the revelation of God in Jesus—God's will, God's nature, God's action, God's plan revealed fully in Jesus—change how followers of Jesus read the Bible?

That is the question behind this book. For the God we meet in Jesus is missional—sent out and on the move—to bring salvation to the world. That God turns all our carefully constructed systems of power and authority upside down by redefining "lordship" as self-emptying, sacrificial love. That God hopes for the salvation of all people and intends to redeem the cosmos. The God revealed in Jesus is above all else a hospitable God, reaching out to religious insiders and outsiders alike with love, forgiveness, and newness of life.

A missional reading of Scripture is pivotal to helping the church find its way back to its true vocation, and to helping newly forming missional communities follow the triune God revealed in Jesus. To the extent that the church is absorbed with itself and its own comfort and agendas it has forsaken the God revealed in Jesus, whom we claim to follow.

Recently a construction worker asked me, "This might sound weird, but do you think maybe the New Testament is God's way of apologizing for the Old Testament?" Noting my puzzled expression, he went on to say, "What I mean is, I think the Old Testament is more of a record of how people thought God was, but most of the time they got it wrong. They thought God was angry and violent, because they were angry and violent. They blamed God for their own shit, interpreted God as if he was just like them. Then Jesus came and he wasn't like that at all. The New Testament was God's way of saying, 'Hey, people! Listen up! You got it all wrong! I'm not like that! I'm like Jesus.'"

As the construction worker intuited, and Brian McLaren has written in *A New Kind of Christianity*, the Bible is, among other things, a library of the way people have thought about God over many thousands of years. What is wondrous to me is that despite all the ways we have gotten it wrong about God in our interpretations, from Genesis to Revelation there are stories of a God who is just like Jesus. These "alternative readings" of God are there for us if we have eyes to see and ears to hear. These texts and ways of reading are exactly what we need today.

The book you are currently holding is the product of several years of collaboration, field-testing, and careful revision by a community of people dedicated to just this sort of reading. My colleague in the Missional Wisdom Foundation, Dr. Bret Wells, and I began this project in 2013 as a practical solution to a specific need. We had been having a difficult time finding an appropriate text for a course in our two-year program, The Academy for Missional Wisdom (now called Launch & Lead). That course, "Reading the Bible with a Missional Church," needed more than just an academic discussion of missional theology or scriptural interpretation. It needed something that modeled a robust theology in an accessible style, and presented in a manner that could help our students envision new possibilities. After several unsuccessful attempts to find just the right book, we decided instead to write a series of essays ourselves.

Those initial essays, and their various revisions, were used in the course for several years. Eventually, however, it became apparent that this project needed to be expanded into a published resource and shared more broadly. I am very pleased that Bret has taken his essays, expanded them, added a few others, and invited contribution from the rest of the MWF Lead Team.

Foreword

This book demonstrates, and invites us to participate in, reading and meditating on representative texts of the Bible from Genesis to Revelation with Jesus looking over our shoulder, so to speak. I believe that by practicing with these few texts we will get better at reading the Bible in light of the missional God revealed in Jesus. When we come to a text that casts God as a bloodthirsty tyrant, we will ask Jesus to show us what it means. When it seems that the men count and the women do not, we will invite Jesus to help us read the text.

This is not a book about critical exegesis or inductive Bible study, nor is it an academic study of the Bible riddled with footnotes from professional scholars. Lord knows, we already have plenty of books like that. Rather it is a meditative reading of several passages of Scripture, informed by missional understandings of God and the church. For rigorous texts about reading the Bible with a missional lens and the relationship of missional hermeneutics to ecclesiology, I recommend the work of Christopher Wright and Ched Myers.[4]

Despite the church's long history of biblical interpretations of God that have been too often violent, patriarchal, racist and exclusive, we are convinced that the real God is hospitable, present, loving, good willed toward humanity, wondrously creative, and determined to heal the cosmos. We believe this about God because of Jesus in the gospels. We believe Jesus is the interpretive key to the rest of the Christian Bible.[5]

With Jesus in the gospels looking over our shoulders, in the following pages you will be invited to consider reading several familiar (and not so familiar) stories of the Bible with "missional eyes." I pray that this volume will help all of us grow closer to Jesus, who always compels us to join in with God's mission in the world, empowered by the Holy Spirit.

—Elaine A. Heath

---

4. Wright, *Mission of God* and *Mission of God's People*. For Ched Myers' biography, books, and other resources, see http://www.chedmyers.org.

5. For more on this topic, see Flood, *Disarming Scripture*.

Preface

THE QUESTION SEEMS SIMPLE enough. In fact, that is precisely why it is so popular—it is simple and safe, an obvious conversation starter: "What do you do?"

And yet . . .

Sitting here in what has been one of my favorite office spaces for nearly ten years—a booth at the Denny's in Burleson, Texas—I can recall many times when that innocuous little question has proven quite difficult to answer.

Of course, it wasn't always this way. The response was relatively straightforward during my years as a minister in more traditional congregations.

"What do you do?"

"I'm a preacher."

"Oh . . . Sorry, if I'd known, I would have watched my language."

"I have several prepared responses to that statement. Which one would you prefer?"

Things became slightly more complex in 2008 when my family stepped into the world of church planting. Other than the occasional need for a definition, "church planter" isn't necessarily a complicated concept.

"What do you do?"

"I'm a church planter."

"A what now?"

"A church planter. It's like a missionary without a passport."

However, our desire to pursue faith—and ecclesiology—via a missional paradigm often required a good deal more explaining.

Preface

"So, where does your church meet?"
"Mostly in the living room."
"Really? In your living room? Why?"
"Probably because that's where we put the food."

We were organized as a network of house churches with many—but not all—of those small communities participating together in a larger worship gathering in a rented space on Sundays. A good deal of my own work was centered around a ministry of presence; spending consistent and considerable time in public spaces like Denny's and local coffee shops, getting to know people as I worked on tasks such as lesson planning, coaching, and writing.

As it turns out, the choice to spend most of my time in coffee shops was one of my more brilliant decisions—though, admittedly, it was accidental brilliance. My interactions and observations in these spaces have taught me more about ministry and how to be part of a community than I have ever picked up in a seminary classroom or sanctuary.

Despite my best efforts, I have gotten to know a lot of people in these spaces over the past decade.[6] Some of those people have become good friends. Many of the relationships naturally evolved into significant discipleship experiences—again, often no thanks to me.[7] I am so grateful for the numerous opportunities I have had to listen to, and walk alongside, a "jaded, post-Christian" friend as they worked through deep wounds and unresolved anger toward churches and Christians. I'm still not the hyper-extroverted "never met a stranger" type, but thanks to these folks I have slowly come to realize I don't have to be.

Just when I started to get a sense for what it was I was doing—which is relatively important in terms of being able to tell

---

6. I was under the impression that wearing both earbuds and keeping your gaze focused on a computer screen was universally understood as, "I'm totally not approachable."

7. I am not quite sure how to describe the experience of having an atheist with a well-documented and deeply rooted distrust of Christians call me out for not speaking more about my faith. But I can certainly say that it was transformative.

someone else what I was doing—it became apparent that things were about to change. I realized unless I drastically altered the focus of my work in our community, or dedicated significantly more of my time to fundraising, I was most likely not going to earn a sustainable income as a church planter. This presented something of a challenge in that neither of those alternative approaches were appealing to me in the slightest.

"What do you do?"
"I hang out at Denny's."
"Wow. Does that pay well?"
"Oh, goodness, no."
"Really? That is surprising."

I also realized that our "network of house churches" approach wasn't suited—financially or philosophically—to bring in additional seminary-trained clergy to lead new communities. There was a much bigger issue at stake than just my personal finances.

For that reason, I began working on a doctor of ministry degree at the Perkins School of Theology at Southern Methodist University with the goal of developing processes for training people to lead missional communities in their own local context. That is where I met Dr. Elaine Heath and learned that she and Larry Duggins had recently begun plans to form the Missional Wisdom Foundation (MWF).

The Missional Wisdom Foundation

Drawing on her work as a professor with Perkins students and her experiences as an elder in the United Methodist Church, Dr. Heath had come to many of the same conclusions I had reached about the need for, and the practical realities of, alternative forms of Christian community. She saw that the intensely local, contextual, and "all of us together" missional paradigm called for new approaches to theological education and leadership training. To this end, Heath and Duggins began developing what would become the MWF's first two community experiments: the Epworth Project, and The People of New Day.

Preface

Epworth houses are short-term, residential forms of intentional Christian community, where people have an opportunity to experience life together, ordered around a shared rule of life and commitment to service and hospitality in their neighborhood.

New Day is a simple form of worshipping community, typically operating in a house-church format, led by a—usually unpaid—team of individuals who follow a rule of life together and share the responsibilities of leadership. The worship itself is simple and intentionally reflects the culture and context in which it emerges.

During this same period, I continued exploring paths and best practices through my studies at SMU and in our local church planting context, and we began developing The Academy for Missional Wisdom (AMW). In 2011, we began our first two cohorts of this two-year program[8] that equips individuals and teams to launch and lead alternative forms of Christian community and/or work with those who do.

The work was exciting, creative, exhausting, and not always easy to describe. It was also not doing very much to keep the bills paid. In order to continue pursuing this meaningful and significant—but financially draining—work, I began picking up part-time jobs that offered flexible schedules.

"What do you do?"

"I don't understand the question. What do I do when? You're going to have to be more specific."

When I began working as the first, extremely part-time, paid employee for the MWF in 2011, I had a total of six different "jobs." If you had asked me during that time, I undoubtedly would have guessed—and hoped—this was about as complicated of a "What do you do?" scenario as I was likely to experience.

Then the Missional Wisdom Foundation really started gaining traction.

Though it took us an embarrassingly long time to be able to state it this clearly, from the very beginning the MWF has experimented with and taught about alternative forms of Christian

---

8. Now known as Launch & Lead.

community. I doubt anyone was more relieved than me once we stumbled on this simple description. Finally, a coherent response.

"What do you do?"

"I help lead a non-profit that experiments with and teaches about alternative forms of Christian community."

"Why do I have the feeling that every word in that sentence represents the starting point of an entire paragraph?"

"Because, imaginary interlocutor, you are quite perceptive."

We take both sides of this equation—experimenting and teaching—seriously, and have been blessed with many opportunities to be creative and innovative in our pursuit of each. MWF currently employs just under thirty employees, spread across the United States. Additionally, there are many others who are not on the payroll, but who are partnered with us in vast array of amazing and collaborative efforts.

Most of the individuals who are part of the Missional Wisdom Foundation had a similar entry point. Simply put, God had been preparing them for just such a time as this. Our community is comprised of story after story of people who had been dreaming, longing, hoping, and looking for something they felt called to pursue, but often couldn't quite express in words. Then one day they had a seemingly "chance encounter" with MWF people or projects. Very often not only had the individual been looking for just something like this, but MWF had been needing someone just like them.

For instance:

Because of relationships established through New Day, several people within MWF began exploring options for an economic empowerment project to support the difficult cultural transition experienced by African refugees. The idea of a sewing collective seemed to be a perfect fit, but it wasn't clear how we would effectively provide the leadership and training to develop such an endeavor. Then we happened to meet an individual with a degree and work experience in textile manufacturing—a person who just happened to be looking for ways to use her skills to benefit others.

Preface

Almost every one of us can tell a similar story of how we came to be part of this community. The same can be said not only for the people, but also for many of our different experiments and programs.

For instance:

An MWF employee, tired of working from home, decides to join a brand new co-working space in Dallas, and almost immediately realizes the potential connection between co-working and missional community. Sometime later, the pastor of a congregation with declining membership expresses an interest in creating something like a co-working space in their underused church building. MWF and White Rock UMC begin exploring the possibility of renovating their basement for just such a purpose. A couple years later, The Mix CoWorking and Creative Space is now a thing that exists.[9]

The MWF has now been able to lead multiple successful experiments in reimaging and transitioning semi-abandoned church spaces; cultivating an authentic and positive presence in the community while still maintaining worship space for the original congregation.

Through firsthand engagement we have discovered important lessons, insights, and pitfalls to share with those who hope to do something similar, and have developed creativity-inspiring demonstration plots for those who are beginning to wonder if different forms of community are possible. Beyond that, these encounters have served to challenge, expand, and refine our theological understandings; we have come to more fully appreciate and view community as a means of grace.[10]

Regardless of whether one believes in "coincidence," these serendipitous encounters have become entirely too common to be dismissed as happenstance. In fact, these experiences are so much

---

9. To be clear, with that innocuous sounding "a couple years later," I am referring to the combined efforts, countless hours, persistence in the face of frustrating setbacks, and many inspiring stories of a dedicated and talented team of people.

10. See Duggins, *Together*.

a part of our story, we have a phrase to describe them: Holy Spirit efficiency.

The cohorts and community of participants in our educational programs reflect the same beautiful, messy, and hard-to-fully-describe web of stories, hopes, and experiences that forms the core of MWF. Since the beginning of the Academy of Missional Wisdom/Launch & Lead, there has been a mixture of clergy and laity, young and less-young, professors and students, those with tremendous experience in missional church leadership and those who have only recently discovered the word *missional*.

We have met people who:

- hope to plant a church
- have already started and are leading a network of house churches
- want to form and experience intentional Christian community
- intend to start a community-focused ministry in their established congregation
- seek to start a non-profit that battles systemic injustice or addresses issues of community development
- are searching for ways to reclaim and cultivate the elusive concepts of neighborhood and community, but not necessarily as the beginning of a new church, nor as a formal ministry of an existing congregation
- have felt a deep resonance with the people and communities connected to the MWF, inspiring them to . . . something.

With such a diverse community of learners representing an equally diverse set of goals and intentions, finding textbooks for courses can be a challenge. This challenge is mitigated somewhat through our focus on the process over product, which we will address in the first chapter of this book.

There was, however, one course that consistently resisted our combined attempts to find an appropriate text: Reading the Bible with a Missional Church. Following several failed attempts to find the right book, Elaine and I decided to "be the change we wanted to see." Rather than continue looking for the perfect book, the two of us wrote a series of essays that covered passages of Scripture throughout the Hebrew Scriptures and the New Testament. For the past five years, Launch & Lead participants have read and discussed those essays in their coursework.

Reading the Bible with a Missional Church

Over the years, our students have offered valuable feedback that helped me revise and refine my initial essays. Others—notably, our incredibly talented editor, Andrea Lingle—have provided insight and guidance in developing additional chapters and content. Likewise, my friends and co-laborers on the MWF Lead Team—Larry Duggins, Denise Crane, and Heidi Miller—were gracious enough to lend their voices to this conversation. This book represents the ongoing work and collaboration of our community.

Following an introduction to the background, intentions, and theological foundations of this book in chapter 1, the rest of the book progresses through a series of meditative readings on various passages of Scripture.

Chapter 2 explores the question, "What kind of God is God?" by considering the picture of God painted for us in the first two chapters of Genesis. From the very beginning we will notice how our questions and assumptions about God naturally influence—and are all too often influenced by—our assumptions about humanity and God's relationship with Creation.

Chapter 3 highlights stories spanning from the final chapters of Genesis all the way through the reign of King David in 2 Samuel. Among other things, Israel's story demonstrates God's persistent desire to cultivate true community with humanity. Contrary to depictions of "the God of Old Testament" as vengeful and unyieldingly focused on perfect rule following, story after story describe a God who is gentle, compassionate, and patient with the Israelites' struggle to embrace their identity. This God would rather set up a tent among the people—to be on the move with them—than to be ensconced in an impressive temple and kept at arm's length.

Chapter 4 picks up the story in the final chapters of Isaiah, just as people are returning to Jerusalem following the Babylonian captivity. The prophet's words provide an important sign post for any who are seeking to reclaim their identity following a long season of abuse. In the midst of the painful and complex process of rebuilding not just a city, but an entire society; at a time when many religious leaders were advocating rigid legalism and even violence in the name of faithfulness and purity, Isaiah declares that Israel's identity is bound up in their willingness to show compassion for others and to embrace true hospitable community.

As we transition from the Hebrew Scriptures to the New Testament, Larry Duggins and Heidi Miller offer an Interlude on Jesus. Through three different passages—the story of Jesus and the bleeding woman, of Jesus and the woman at the well, and the Christ Hymn in Philippians 2—we are encouraged to pause and consider not only what kind of God we find revealed in Jesus, but how that revelation shapes our story and our identity.

The stories we choose to tell; the aspects of the story we emphasize and upon which we dwell have incredible power to shape and transform. Chapter 5 continues this theme with another passage from Philippians—and an incredibly nerdy metaphor.

In chapter 6 we explore the enigmatic final book of the New Testament. Woven in a tapestry of vibrant colors and epic imagery, Revelation is packed with subtle and decidedly not-so-subtle reassurances about what kind of God we serve. These reminders often come in the form of references to imagery from Israel's past—some of which is described in passages we will have read together.

Chapter 7 looks back across the various discussions, once more returning to our theme of reading the Bible with a missional church, and the conviction that our questions are best explored in community.

I encourage you to slow down and look at these familiar (or unfamiliar) passages carefully. Watch closely, notice what is going on around, and don't be afraid to ask: What kind of God is God?

1

What Does It All Mean?

> Within this story, as narrated or anticipated by the Bible, there is at work the God whose mission is evident from creation to new creation.
> This is the story of God's mission.
>
> —Christopher J. H. Wright[1]

Missional.

For many, the word *missional* has become like the latest hit song on a pop music radio station: love it or hate it, you can't go ten minutes without hearing it . . . and you catch yourself singing along unconsciously. Or perhaps Apple secretly owns the word. It shows up in front of nearly everything—in the way of their lower-case "i."

Speaking of which, yes, there is an iMissional.org.

Everywhere we look folks are slapping *missional* on programs that used to be called emergent, contemporary, progressive, or whatever screams relevant and cutting edge. Sometimes it almost seems the word has no real meaning at all—it's just the latest buzzword.

The Missional Wisdom Foundation does not believe that is the case. At the very least, that is not how we're using the word.[2]

---

1. Wright, *Mission of God,* loc. 491–92.
2. Which, I suppose, is probably what anyone who uses the word would say.

Missional refers to something meaningful and important for the church. Like the gospel itself, the word missional refers to something robust and complex, but also incredibly simple.

The simple definition of *missional* is "sent." To use the label *missional church* is to suggest that the whole church exists as a community sent with God. *Missional* should be an unnecessary and redundant descriptor, and we long for a day when it makes sense to simply stop using the word. However, at this moment, it offers the church a vital reminder of its calling, purpose, and identity. It is "helping the church be the church."[3]

Beginning Our Journey of Discovery

This opening chapter provides context, background, and a description of the book's project. For the sake of clarity, we will define and briefly unpack how we're using terms like *missional*, and *the mission of God*, and even give some specific explanation regarding a *missional hermeneutic* (which, if you don't know the term, just means our method for reading and interpreting the Bible).

We have often been asked how a missional mindset or perspective impacts the way we read Scripture. Sometimes people want to know how we interpret a particular passage or how we believe the Bible might speak to a specific issue in the contemporary landscape. Some people are curious about the efficacy of the missional perspective. Others have doubts about its validity. And then there are those who still aren't sure what *missional* actually means. And yet, in one way or another, they are all wanting to know what it means, and how the Bible speaks to and through a missional life.

Often, the search to understand is a search to define—with specifics and details, including concrete lists and examples. The Enlightenment and modernity have convinced us that we can understand anything with enough information. To truly know that which we are studying, we simply need to break it down to its most basic components. We find truth by analyzing the individual pieces of the puzzle.

---

3. Wilson-Hartgrove, *New Monasticism*, 21.

This strategy can yield tremendous insight and discovery in the right context. It is certainly helpful for reverse engineering an unfamiliar machine or new technology (provided that the person doing the dismantling is somewhat familiar with how machines function). And yet, for all the benefits we have gained from the Enlightenment, its core assumptions are insufficient on their own. There is more to understanding than merely analyzing, cataloging, and blueprinting.

When a largely abstract concept is reduced to specific expressions and detailed lists, the discernment process can be short-circuited. We are tempted to forgo the time-consuming process of discerning the specifics of our own context, in favor of replicating what others have done.

Following a generic plan may seem like an efficient and responsible way to be more collaborative and avoid the isolationist tendency to "reinvent the wheel." However, if we aren't careful, we miss the vital fact that what made those specifics successful was the situation in which they came to fruition; successful actions are often an outcome and expression of a process of deep discernment within a particular context.

From this perspective we begin to see that the define-and-prescribe approach is not an efficient path to understanding at all. It can narrow our vision and inhibit critical and creative thinking. This approach can inadvertently cause us to become attuned to—and consequently, limited by—the details provided rather than teaching us how to look for evidence of God at work around us. It may take more time initially, but we will be better served by participating in and learning from the process itself—more so than the specific product it generated.[4]

In our experience, one of the best ways to shift the emphasis from the product to the process is found in the adage, "Show, don't tell." That is why, as often as possible, when we are asked what a missional stance looks like in practice, our response is simply, "Come and see." In this way, we invite people into an experience;

---

4. Perhaps a subtle foreshadowing of how we teach people to move from theory to practice? Nah, that would be too obvious.

into the midst of a process that transcends any particular outcome or product.

That is precisely the invitation we offer with this book: Come, read with us, and see.

Missional, the Mission of God, and Why Anyone Should Care

We do believe those who are committed to (or even just considering) missional and incarnational[5] approaches to faith should wrestle with the biblical and theological principles behind them. To be sure, the missional posture leads to very effective ways of "doing church" and being a disciple. And yet, effectiveness is not our primary motivation for embracing a missional approach to faith, because in the most basic sense, *missional* isn't about what we do at all—at least, not initially.

Missional is first a *theological*, rather than pragmatic, strategic, or marketing concept. It is rooted in our encounter with the Trinitarian God, modeled in the text of Scripture, witnessed in the life of the early church, and evident throughout our history.

Theology is the practice of thinking about, contemplating, and exploring our understanding of God. So, when we say this is a theological issue, our claim is that to speak about something as missional is to say something about God—not just the strategies, practices, or attitudes of Christians.

The mission we refer to in the word *missional* is God's mission, not ours. The one who created this world and everything in it is also the one who has come near to reconcile, heal, and restore. The *missio dei*, or *mission of God*, is a phrase that points to everything God is doing to redeem and reconcile creation, and *missional*

---

5. These two terms are often used in tandem. To be incarnational is to be fully and deeply present. As Alan Hirsch has said, "If God is a sending God, incarnational is how God sends." For both a brief video and written description of Hirsch's take on the "Missional-Incarnational Impulse," see http://www.vergenetwork.org/2010/10/02/alan-hirsch-missional-incarnational-impulse/ (accessed December 15, 2015).

refers to our existence as people who have been called together and sent out to join in the mission of God.

The mission of God leads us to confront the injustices in our society, shed light on the lies we tell ourselves, and name the sickness in our midst. These issues exist in every context, so every context is an appropriate place to address these issues. This means, wherever you are, you are already in a place where the mission of God is at work. Every place where people live and move and have their being is a place where people are loved by God and should be loved by the people of God.

None of these contexts should be abandoned by the church.

The call to discern the specifics of God's mission in our own context is in no way a free pass to remain tucked away in our comfort zones and relative security. Rather, it is a reminder that "if real life with God can happen anywhere at all, it can happen here, among the people whose troubles are already evident to us."[6]

Of course, this assumes we're paying enough attention to the people we are among that their troubles *are* evident to us and that ours are to them. We must not be content to ignore those troubles or shake our self-satisfied heads in judgment of people who have clearly brought their troubles on themselves.

Some of us will need to resist overlooking the troubles plaguing individuals and families in our seemingly boring, suburban, "nothing to see here" neighborhoods. If we desire real life with God, we are encouraged to cultivate real life *with* the people around us. This is, of course, difficult to accomplish if we know nothing *about* the people around us.

The Epworth Project, a ministry of the Missional Wisdom Foundation, demonstrates one way in which people are attempting to pursue real life with God by cultivating community with others. Dr. Elaine Heath was inspired to start this experiment in intentional Christian community after numerous seminary students approached her expressing a frustrated longing for a deeper experience of both ministry and spiritual formation. In the Epworth Project, residents are invited to spend a few years cultivating

---

6. Wilson-Hartgrove, *Wisdom of Stability*, 24.

and living in missional, monastic community with others. People in these houses live under a communal rule of life and commit to engaging the mission of God in their local community. Some of these houses focus on ministry with the homeless or the working poor. Others are engaged in life and service alongside refugees and struggling minority populations.

There is not, however, a predetermined list of topics or issues from which Epworth houses are expected to choose their ministry focus. The specific mission of a house is determined by the residents, as they pay attention to the prompting of the Holy Spirit, listen to the hopes and concerns of their neighbors, and consider their own passions and callings. Through this posture of listening and participation, the residents discern the neighborhood together, and discover—rather than manufacture—the house's mission.[7]

There is no predetermined list of topics, because such a list would be too vast to compile. Participating in the mission of God includes evangelism, salvation, justice, hospitality, generosity, forgiveness, proclamation, and presence. When we speak of mission, we're talking about introducing people to the person and the way of Jesus and we're talking about working for social justice. We're talking about love instead of apathy. We're talking about joining people as they search for pathways out of backbreaking poverty; sharing our food with the hungry and our clothes with the naked; caring for the weak, the forgotten, the overlooked, and the marginalized. We mean loving our neighbor—not just recruiting them.

It also means opening ourselves to receiving these gifts from the neighborhood, rather than assuming we come with the solution or the answer. We come to hear, appreciate, and perhaps add our voices to the chorus. We come to pour out, but also to be filled.

This is about anticipating, longing for, and practicing the full arrival of God's kingdom—a community where greed, selfishness, isolation, coercive power, tyranny, and oppressive control will be eradicated. We're talking about life instead of death, hope instead

---

[7]. If you're interested in forming this sort of community, we encourage you to check out: Heath, *Abide*. The book and accompanying DVD curriculum are available online at www.mishwiz.com.

of despair, light instead of darkness. We're talking about compassion, hospitality, and tearing down barriers that separate us.

We're talking about whatever it is that God is up to in our neighborhoods, our towns, our state, our country, our continent, our hemisphere, our world, and our universe. We're talking about things beyond us; things which we cannot begin to fully comprehend but for which we keep our eyes open. We're talking about every good, noble, pure, excellent, and praiseworthy thing that God is doing and in which we are being invited to join. We are talking about whatever God allows us (and you) to engage in for the good of God's Kingdom.

The specifics exist in context, not theory.

The mission of God involves the church, challenges our inconsistencies, and cultivates worshipping-community. But it doesn't stop there. The mission of God is at work anywhere there is brokenness, pain, and suffering; anywhere that God's will is not yet done on earth as it is in heaven.

In short, *mission* includes everything that God is doing everywhere. And we humans, created in God's image, are invited to participate as co-creators. This is who we were created to be.

We live this way, on mission with God, because we are people of God. In this way, our actions are in response to our calling, and thus originate not in our own awesomeness but in the Divine Awesomitude. We can't really claim to *be* these people if we refuse to *do* what such people are called to do—but doing is a result of being, not the other way around.

The missional orientation elicits a tangible response from disciples of Jesus; this is not merely an academic philosophy. Though it carries a significant call to active faith, *missional* is *who we are* more than a specific list describing *what we do*. Yes, it involves a call to be answered with our intellect, our emotions, and most certainly our actions; however, it cannot be stressed enough that *missional* is more than an adjective to be placed alongside a program, model, or pragmatic list of activities.

Missional transcends a call to personal piety, activism, social justice, evangelism, or discipleship—it encompasses all these aspects in a holistic call to the way of Jesus, empowered by the Spirit, amid God's work in this place . . . together, as the body of Christ.

Each disciple of Jesus, each person who bears the name "Christian," is included in this call—not just those who attended seminary, have tons of free time to volunteer, enjoy teaching Sunday school, set aside time in the summer for a mission trip to Mexico, or consider themselves an extrovert.

It makes a great deal of sense to look carefully at the relationship between missional theology and Scripture because the Bible is a missional text. When we refer to the Bible as a missional text we're claiming that the Scriptures offer a grand narrative about a missional God who creates as an act of love and hospitality. The brokenness and separation experienced in creation are not God's doing—they are precisely that which God is *undoing* and remaking. As those created in God's image, God is (and has been all along) inviting humanity to collaborate as co-creators in this mission of reconciliation. This is God's mission—and we are called to participate.

One of the primary purposes of Scripture is to equip God's people as those being called and sent together. This story, like all truly great stories, aims to change those who hear it. But our transformation extends beyond ourselves: we are being pulled into the story that transforms everything.

Reading the Bible with (and as) a missional church means we approach the Bible with the assumption that God is actually up to something in this world. We are all called to play an active role in that something, and the Bible is the story of that something.

Why does any of this matter? Does it change anything in real life? Does it help us, or just give us another context for rambling speeches, blog posts, and new books?

Yes. We've already stated our conviction that *missional* is a theological principle rather than a strategy for church planting, church renewal, or something else. It is a vital component for understanding the revealed nature of God. This principle helps us address what we see in the relationship of the Trinity, the calling of

Israel, and the formation of the church. It helps us recognize that the incarnation wasn't a new thing for God, but the seminal expression of how God has been operating since the act of creation.

When a missional church reads the Bible as a missional text, it becomes very difficult to continue viewing faith as an individualistic and privatized practice. We are confronted with our tendency to describe discipleship in terms of membership (and that, merely in terms of attendance and contribution). We no longer treat discipleship, ministry, and mission as extra-credit, or as premium features available as in-app purchases.

This topic matters because too often we've missed how, from beginning to end, the Bible shows us how God is making space for others, pursuing those others to invite them into that space, and then calling those others to become agents of that same space-making adventure.

A missional engagement with Scripture matters because it reminds us that we do not read as detached voyeurs. We are invited into the Story as active participants—even if we considered ourselves outsiders when we started reading.

This way of approaching the Bible matters because all too often we have been quick to view the Scriptures as a list of ways to keep people out, keep ourselves in, and feel good about doing so. And, honestly, it matters because it grounds our sending in something more substantial and sustaining than a fleeting desire for activism.

The Power and Importance of Story

I am a Texan.

I try to be a lovable one, though I confess deriving an odd pleasure in playing out exaggerated versions of some of the more obnoxious stereotypes. It's interesting how easily people will accept something that fits a stereotype, even if it contradicts everything else they know to be true about a person.

I sometimes tell people I have lived in five states: Central Texas, West Texas, South Texas, North Texas, and for a short season,

Louisiana—or, Far East Texas. My time outside of the United States of Texas came when I worked with a church in Mandeville, just across the lake from New Orleans. I was initially hired on a one-year contract to serve as an Outreach Minister following Hurricane Katrina.

The congregation had celebrated the opening of their brand-new church building a week before the storm. Although most people agreed that it looked a lot like a warehouse inside—and not in the trendy way—it turned out to be perfect. The building wasn't damaged in the storm or the flooding, and its spaciousness made it a perfect staging ground for donated supplies and location for housing volunteers.

When the donations and volunteers continued streaming in long after the storm had blown itself out the church began to feel the weight of organizing and tracking follow-up in the area. Even with the help of so many volunteers (many of whom left jobs and family behind for months on end), this church, like many others in the region, shouldered a great deal of responsibility during that time. Some wondered if they could maintain the energy required to continue moving forward in the "new normal" of the post-Katrina Gulf Coast. It should come as no surprise, and without any cause for condemnation, that the members of this relatively small congregation were exhausted and began looking for someone to help the helpers.

That's how, one evening, sitting in my living room in Dallas, Texas, I received a phone call from a preacher in south Louisiana. He had been given my name as someone with experience in disaster relief ministry—specifically in relation to Hurricane Katrina and New Orleans—and wondered if I would be interested in serving for one year as an Outreach Minister.

Upon hearing about the conversation, my normally risk-averse wife—who, incidentally, had given birth to our second son only a few weeks before—did not hesitate before replying, "You know you have to take this job, right? This is obviously what the past few months have been preparing us to do."

What Does It All Mean?

Surprising though her response may have been, there was no denying her point. It was certainly true that I had come through an unexpected immersion in disaster relief work. Just a few days before Hurricane Katrina struck, I had been laid off from a church in Dallas for budget reasons. "Downsized by the Man," sounds a bit more cosmically ominous when you're a minister.

It is easier to joke about now, but this was an incredibly traumatic experience for us. There was nothing resembling "guaranteed appointment" in our faith tradition, and in one conversation, our world had been turned upside down. I lost my job. I lost my health insurance. I lost my church family. I effectively lost (at least, lost close contact with) most of my friends and support network. To make matters more terrifying, my wife and I had just announced that she was pregnant, and that our toddler was going to be a big brother.

But, on the bright side, when Katrina hit, I was in a great position to help start (on a volunteer basis) a nonprofit ministry serving families in the Red Cross evacuation shelter at Reunion Arena in Dallas, Texas.

Nobody was ready for the devastation brought about by Katrina, Rita, and the broken levees. Dallas was no exception. Rosemary Mote, who has worked with the Red Cross for many years, said, "Prior to Katrina, the largest shelter we had operated in North Texas was about 130 people and it was for a hurricane in the late 80s, Gilbert."[8] That certainly changed with Katrina.

"On August 29, 2005, there were 11 people in the Red Cross shelter. By the next night, there were 500 people. And by the third night, we were opening Reunion Arena. And then the day after that was the Dallas Convention Center."[9]

The Red Cross eventually opened a dozen different shelters across North Texas, housing even more than the originally estimated 25,000 evacuees. Reunion Arena hosted around a thousand people and still ended up being one of the smallest North Texas shelters.

8. Collins, "How North Texas Sheltered 26,000 Katrina Evacuees."
9. Austin, "Lessons from Katrina."

WHAT KIND OF GOD?

While nothing like the terrible conditions at the Super Dome in New Orleans or even those at the Dallas Convention Center, the unprecedented size and scope of people's needs understandably created numerous problems at Reunion Arena. People's cots (and whatever possessions they had with them) were on the ground floor, but all the services were up on the chaotic and crowded mezzanine level. That meant while parents were attempting to secure housing, enroll children in school, locate lost relatives, get medical care, file insurance claims, and deal with any number of logistical concerns, they often had little choice but to leave their children unattended—or barely attended by over-extended volunteers—on the ground floor.

That shouldn't be taken as a criticism or a slight against anyone. Everyone was doing the best they could with what they had available—but it was still something that needed to be addressed.

My friend, Shawn Small, heard about the situation. Shawn's nonprofit organization, Wonder Voyage,[10] takes groups of teens and adults on pilgrimages and mission trips all over the world—including New Orleans. Because of his established relationships and his organization's reputation, he was asked to put together a safe place for children to hang out from 8:00 a.m. to 9:00 p.m. each day.

Knowing about my new, extremely flexible, (non)work schedule, Shawn called me around noon on Friday, September 2, and said, "Look. Not to be insensitive, but I know you've got some free time right now . . ."

Five of us arrived at the shelter by 3:00 p.m. After talking with the shelter director, we decided that I would work to lead things at Reunion Arena and he would handle all the offsite operations—including the time-consuming work of lining up groups of volunteers with appropriate background checks. We went home and started calling friends and family for help over the weekend.

The next couple months passed in a whirlwind of activity: watching kids, orienting volunteers, fighting red tape, reacting to (and eventually learning to anticipate) problems in an

---

10. www.wondervoyage.com.

ever-changing environment, and sitting on cots listening to mothers and fathers. It was common for people to say, "I need to tell this story to someone who wasn't there. The others won't really listen because they have their own Katrina story they're trying to tell."

A couple days after the shelter closed I stumbled into an opportunity to work as an independent insurance adjuster for storm-related homeowner's claims in—you guessed it—New Orleans. Two months of volunteer work at Reunion Arena had eaten away a significant chunk of my severance package. I still didn't have a job, so I agreed—and a few days later I was navigating through a post-apocalyptic landscape that can't possibly be described in a few sentences. At that time, New Orleans was still largely abandoned and locked-down, so we stayed in an RV park outside of Baton Rouge—where I spent my evenings frantically learning the claim submission system and finishing up my final semester of grad school (online, obviously).

Each morning we loaded up our gear and drove into what used to be a thriving city. No words can express the surreal experience of navigating around in that destruction. We had to rely on GPS, because maps didn't correlate to the new landscape. We would pull up to an address and find the house missing, only to realize it was the building sitting in the intersection a block away. Did you know, after carrying it down the street, flood waters can deposit your house at just the right angle so that a chain link fence will hold it (your house) up without it (the fence) being crushed?

Even though New Orleans is a big city, there were days when we didn't see another human being other than the occasional soldier standing at a National Guard checkpoint or driving around in a Humvee. There were days when I met with homeowners who were still in the area or who were close enough to drive back for an appointment. Usually this was the first time they had been allowed back into the city to even see what happened.

Often those days involved standing silently—or crying and praying—with them in what used to be their front yard or living room. As I had found myself doing on numerous cots on the arena floor, I often spent time listening as they told their stories. Many of these people had been able to tell their story to people who couldn't even imagine the devastation. Now they needed someone to listen while also bearing witness to the tragedy.

During my time at the shelter helping families fleeing the storm, my time as an adjuster helping people return (or move on), and my time at the church in Mandeville helping people rebuild (physically, emotionally, and spiritually) I became a witness to their stories. So many people had a deep, almost visceral, need for someone to hear their story; to let them get it out without trying to compare notes with them or hurry them along.

It was sobering and humbling. It was challenging. Some days, it was rewarding. Occasionally, it was soul-crushing and depressing. It was always exhausting, but not always in a bad way.

Perhaps more than anything else, it was transformative. I served a priestly role by listening to the stories of these people, and they served a priestly role by teaching me the importance of doing so.

As I look back on that time, it is easy to notice a glaring deficiency; an ironic twist that eventually led me into a season of despair and dysfunction so deep it took nearly a decade to recover.

When you spend your days sitting on a cot, listening to stories from people who have just lost everything, your own story of losing your job just doesn't seem worth telling. At least, it didn't to me.

When you find yourself standing with people in what used to be their front yard, in front of what used to be their house, you don't really think to say, "You know, I'm having a hard time processing and dealing with some of the stories I heard at Reunion Arena."

When you have been hired by a church—grasping about for fresh reinforcements to provide relief to those who have been shouldering incredible burdens in the aftermath of disaster—well, you're expected to act like a fresh reinforcement. You are not expected to act like another shell-shocked, confused, exhausted person struggling to get out of bed in the morning. Somehow, I was aware of the importance for the people of New Orleans to tell their stories, yet I was blind to how deeply I was experiencing, and burying, that same need.

Without being able to say, and have someone listen as you say, "This is what happened to me," it can be difficult to say, "This is what I'm going to do about it."

There are many reasons people find themselves unable to tell their stories. Perhaps they feel a (real or imagined) sense of illegitimacy and, therefore, pressure to be silent amid more pressing or more significant matters. Some retreat into silence after experiencing resistance, rejection, or reprisal. Perhaps their story threatens to disrupt the status quo or functions as an indictment against those who benefit from the status quo. Others never speak up because they are simply afraid to reveal what's going on behind the carefully constructed mask they show the world.

And sadly, many choose not to speak because they don't want to deal with platitudes and admonitions that, in one way or another, dismiss the value of their story. These cheap words often emerge because the "listener" is uncomfortable and unable or unwilling to simply hold space for the other.

Regardless of why it happens, human beings suffer whenever they feel that they are not heard or cannot tell their story. Not surprisingly, those who experience this type of suffering may also find it very difficult to hear others' stories.

We never come to the text as a blank slate; everyone brings their stories with them. This is both a significant challenge and a tremendous benefit of reading the Bible in community—especially diverse community. And, when we read the Bible, we're not reading a list of context-free propositions, we're encountering stories. For this reason, it is important that we have a healthy appreciation for how our stories can impact our ability to hear the text and one another.

When we read the Bible together in community we have a built-in opportunity to encounter and learn from diverse perspectives. We have a natural reminder to pay attention to how our isolated story may limit our ability to hear. Sadly, we also have a built-in opportunity to ignore, dismiss, or simply leave no room for others' stories.

The invitation to read the Bible with a missional church is an invitation to create space for listening. A space for storytelling. A place for the deeply human, and deeply divine experience of connection.

Like the rabbits in *Watership Down*,[11] the Story sustains us because it reminds us of who we are, why we are, where we come from, and where we are headed. The Story reminds us of those who have come before—both the Divine Traveler and our very much human traveling companions and predecessors.

The Story emboldens, encourages, and refuels us when we are brought low; it reminds us that in both the act of suffering and the experience of beauty we discover kinship and connection with others. We experience the deep connection born of shared struggle with those, living and long dead, who have faced the pain of love in the name of the Community of Love. And, as we consider things too wonderful to describe, rather than casting about for something to say, we can simply share holy space with one another.

The Bible tells us the story of the God of mission. It invites humanity into the mission of God by transforming those who are sent into ambassadors of transformation wherever they go. And this Story serves as light in the darkness urging us to press on toward the sunrise. Do not give up! Do not lose heart! You are not alone!

Story and a Missional Hermeneutic

> A narrative has several characteristics. It comprises a story that is moving somewhere; it gives a social group a story that tells where it is going and what the group will look like when it arrives. There is purpose and quest within the narrative calling a group in a specific direction and toward a particular goal. . . . Because narrative creates and sustains social community, it's the glue, the

11. Adams, *Watership Down*.

atmosphere of all social life. The key to innovating missional community is formation of a people within a specific memory and narrative.

—Alan Roxburgh[12]

The narrative of the Bible, throughout the Hebrew Scriptures and the New Testament, tells the story of God coming near to side with those who are oppressed, whether by tyrants or their own sinfulness, for redemption and reconciliation. This is an enormous mission that transcends our definitions and even our imagination. Recognizing the immensity of the mission of God shouldn't be a source of anxiety or guilt; it should be freeing. God is at work! God is at work beyond us!

There's plenty to do, so we don't have to worry about being bored. There's enough that all disciples everywhere have a role to play and work to do. Neither my little community nor someone else's large one (and certainly not any one of us individually) could ever hope or be expected to join God everywhere in everything.

In response to questions about how we can engage in the mission of God, one might say, "Look out your window. What is God doing there? Ask if you can help." The possibilities are simply too vast for a detailed definition.

For many people, "look out your window" is overwhelming to the point of being unfathomable. "What am I looking for? How do I know what God is doing?" If we are not already experienced in this sort of missional imagination, how do we even begin?

Once again, this is why we try invite people to "come and see." We learn by witnessing, by experiencing, by doing. And yet, this isn't always possible either, at least, not in a physical sense. And that is precisely why story is such a valuable tool.

Story compels us to first step back and consider not just the specific details but the larger picture. This act of stepping back is not a retreat. The practice of storytelling is not an escapist activity. Hearing the stories of God at work in Scripture, in history, and in the lives of our companions is more than nostalgia. The use of

---

12. Roxburgh and Romanuk, *Missional Leader,* 70–71.

story to ignite the missional imagination is an act of prophetic ministry that confronts our complacency and offers invitation to hopeful engagement with our context. Story is so powerful that it can be manipulative, so we take the missional posture seriously by recognizing that the story belongs to the *whole community*. Each of us shares in the responsibility of telling, retelling, and passing it on to new generations of storytellers.

Each of the following chapters seeks to *model*, rather than providing a detailed "how to" manual for, engaging the text of Scripture just as we have briefly described engaging our neighborhood. These pages present an embodied *missional hermeneutic*. A hermeneutic is an approach to reading and understanding. It is the posture one takes in considering a text. We all have a hermeneutic—none of us more so than those who claim they do not! A missional hermeneutic, then, is a way of reading the Bible with the awareness that God is up to something, and we are all being called to join in that something.

In *The Mission of God* Christopher Wright poignantly claims, "A missional hermeneutic proceeds from the assumption that the whole Bible renders to us the story of God's mission through God's people in their engagement with God's world for the sake of the whole of God's creation."[13] A few pages later he continues:

> To read the whole Bible in the light of this great overarching perspective of the mission of God, then, is to read with the grain of this whole collection of texts that constitute our canon of Scripture. . . . It is nothing more than to accept that the biblical worldview locates us in the midst of a narrative of the universe behind which stands the mission of the living God.[14]

---

13. Wright, *Mission of God*, 51.
14. Ibid., 64.

What Does It All Mean?

Developing a Missional Hermeneutic

Before moving on, it would be helpful to provide a little more context for how a missional hermeneutic can orient us toward the texts we're reading. While they will not always be pointed out directly, readers are encouraged to look for the ways that these principles are applied to the various passages addressed in this book.

In the same way that we "read" our neighborhood, George Hunsberger has proposed a holistic vision of approaching the Bible that helps us ask what God is doing.[15] His proposal represents a summary and synthesis of materials offered by numerous people after several years of study, presentations, and debates about what, if anything, constitutes an appropriate missional hermeneutic. Hunsberger noted that over the course of these discussions, papers, and presentations, four distinct streams had emerged. Rather than viewing them in competition as many had done, he suggested they serve complementary roles—developing a much richer context than any one could achieve on its own.

Those four streams are

1. the missional direction of the story;
2. the missional purpose of the story;
3. the missional identity of the recipients;
4. the missional engagement of culture.

The missional direction of the story means that what we encounter in the Bible is an overarching narrative of redemption and reconciliation. This is the story of a God who is on the move: the God of mission. This is what we would call a metanarrative—the larger story within which smaller stories exist as well. That doesn't mean that every individual story will function as a mini-version of the larger trajectory, but each finds its place (and sometimes redemption) within the larger story.

Because we understand that the passages function within a larger scope, we are released from the pressure to find or create

---

15. Hunsberger, "Proposals," 309–21.

a moral or lesson in every chapter. That is a relief because some of the stories are absolutely awful and seem to have very little redeeming value. If you're unsure whether that's accurate, I challenge you to reread the Judah and Tamar story in Genesis (if you're not familiar, Google it . . . but fair warning, it is not safe for work).

Rather than saying each individual narrative is written from the perspective of displaying a "biblical model for a missional [whatever]," this mindset, instead, calls us to see where the bigger picture is headed and to begin imagining what this preferred future will look like. Revelation 21, which we'll discuss later in the book, is a good example.

The second stream, *the missional purpose of the story*, reminds us that not only is there is missional direction at work, but that forming missional disciples is one of the very reasons the stories are told in the first place. Whoever hears these words and puts them into practice will be transformed. As we know, there can be a big difference between hearing the words uttered and actually *hearing the words*. The purpose of the Bible is not simply to provide rules to follow or information to memorize. The purpose is transformation. Being changed, being called and equipped, being transformed by the renewing of our minds; this is the point and the purpose.

The third stream, *the missional identity of the recipients* is to recognize that these texts were written not only about a missional endeavor or to form a missional people, but also with the assumption that the recipients are already understood as being a people sent by God. This is a very common theme in the Bible, and much of the distress and pain in the stories stems from the people forgetting why they were sent—or forgetting they were sent at all.

The Bible's primary audience is not the curious bystander who has no intention of living it out. Over and over the text assumes—and reminds—the readers or hearers of this Word that they have already been called to action. These writings strengthen, equip, empower, and hold accountable a group who needs and desires to live fully on mission with God. As Hunsberger said in his paper, "It is not just our right, but our responsibility as the missional community to read, ask hard questions, come to conclusions, and move forward in faith."

We are the interpreting community. We come to this text with questions that arise from living the message in our whole lives. So, of course we must approach this as a missional text—because we're a missional people, God is a missional God, and this is the story of the relationship between us.

So, these first three streams remind us that to read the Bible as a missional community is to be aware of the missional flow of God's story. But we must also remember that the text is meant to *form* a missional people in addition to *informing* us of a missional God. Furthermore, and sometimes paradoxically, the text is addressed *to* a missional people. This "already, but not yet" dynamic is a common theme in the Bible. The Kingdom of God is at hand, and we are anticipating its arrival. We have been made holy, and we are in the process of being made holy. We are created in the image of God, and we are in the process of being continually conformed to the image of Christ.

The direction, purpose, and identity streams answer questions such as, "Who is this God? What is this book? Why should I read it?" The fourth stream, the *missional engagement with culture*, addresses the question, "So, how do I go about doing that here and now?"

If we want to know how to go about engaging the missional imagination in our context, Scripture itself is ready to point us in the right direction. However, this stream is where we see the value of holding all four in conversation. When we fail to recognize the direction and purpose of the text, and the assumed identity of its readers, it is very easy to misread and misapply Scripture.

So many disputes in the Christian faith, such as the issue of gender equality in church leadership, stem from our failure to realize that the text often (though certainly not always) functions to teach us *how* to engage culture more than describing every detail for what to do.

To use a well-worn phrase, the Bible is teaching us how to fish instead of giving us a fish.

Unfortunately, we often seem to assume that the Bible was written to tell us what to do in every imaginable situation, thus eliminating the need for discernment. Though this may seem like humble reverence that defers to the Bible's authority, in practice it is (often unintentionally) an incredibly narcissistic posture. Reading the Bible in this way puts us, and the specifics of our context, at the center of everything. In doing so, we tend to ignore or diminish what may or may not have been going on in the original recipients' context, as well as how those situations may differ significantly from our own.

In order to keep this point in mind, my father-in-law often reminds people, "When we read the Bible, we need to remember that even though we're invited to do so, we're reading someone else's mail." Beginning with the awareness that we're "reading someone else's mail" doesn't mean that the Bible is not written for us as well, just that it wasn't written to us initially. Far from making the text less relevant to our lives, it helps us focus on why and how these words functioned, which in turn provides wisdom for the why's and how's in our own setting.

A missional reading of Scripture involves intentionally approaching the text to discern how to engage culture—not to skip the discernment process.

The Bible itself, and particularly the gospels, provides us with a matrix for engaging our own culture with the text of Scripture; applying it directly to our context, drawing from our own metaphors, recognizing the uniqueness of this place and this time.

As the missional people of a missional God, it makes sense to read Scripture from a missional perspective. Taken together, these four streams lay out a holistic posture for a missional reading of Scripture. This isn't something we have to use our imagination to find; the text itself carries the mark of the missional life of our community.

To summarize: the text of Scripture presents a missional narrative that is meant to both cultivate and be received by a missional people and provides the proper lens for engaging the surrounding culture.

What Does It All Mean?

Notes from Denise

Missional means "sent." This word has been hijacked by being applied and co-mingled with specific activities where we "help others"—often with little awareness or understanding of who these others are, and whether our actions are even helping—or where we are doing something outside routine "church." It is refreshing to see the word with this simple understanding: sent. And just to consider the possibility of a day in which "missional church" has become a redundant phrase . . . what a beautiful picture!

Understanding is not equal to defining. Something deeper can happen when we let ourselves stop defining, labeling, and categorizing because we are trained to think in a certain way. Instead, to look out and see what God is up to and just get on board, together in community, under the guidance of the Spirit as part of the great Story. How complicated we make that . . .

The story is unfolding. The trajectory is set. Open up and see with a lens that won't necessarily be clear, but can reveal a different point of view. One that can see that "all manner of things shall be well." This book can help re-discover ancient wisdom by clearing away the confusion around contexts and help find the path by walking it.

What if . . . we really read the story this way?

What if . . . we really talked to our neighbor without judgment or agenda?

What if . . . we just looked outside and asked God what He/She/They was up to and how we could get in on the action?

What if . . . we recognized how our story influences were influenced by the Story?

What if . . .

2

Genesis 1–2: The Community of Love

BEFORE THE BEGINNING THERE was Community. God, the Community of Love, which we refer to as the Trinity of Father, Son, and Holy Spirit and, among others, Creator, Redeemer, Sustainer, had a perfect relationship of mutual love and respect. This isn't to say that there are three gods—there is one God and this God is the essence of Love. Love neither exists in, nor is it expressed in, isolation; it is expressed in community.

This God, as a Community of Love, is not incomplete; the Trinity is the definition of completion. Community needs nothing. Love lacks nothing. Love is eternally and completely expressed within the Community of the one God in three persons.

However, while the Community of Love is not incomplete, neither is God static. The nature of true Community is expansive. It is dynamic. It is always growing and bringing into itself everything around it. The relationship of the Community, being rooted and established in a deep, indescribable love, is creative. For that is what love is and what love does. It continually creates opportunity for love to be expressed and to give itself away. It withdraws so that others can exist. Trinitarian love is innately kenotic. It is always pouring out and being poured into, always self-emptying but never emptied.

Genesis 1–2: The Community of Love

In an act of hospitality and true love, the Community of Love created. God brushed away the darkness, stepped into the midst of chaos, and brought forth solid foundations. God molded and formed a magnificent, advancing universe, and in an inconspicuous section began to paint, with beautiful strokes, a landscape that begged to be enjoyed.

The Spirit of the Lord hovered over the chaos—above its tumult and beyond its fury. Pure, limitless power, which not only existed above the chaos, but brought order out from its midst by sheer will. The power of the Community was displayed in the act of speaking. With a Word, life became possible. And yet, since the beginning, the Community has freely chosen to engage, to draw near.

And God walked in the garden.

The Lord knelt and, from the same material that formed mountains, deserts and jungles, the same material that made up the fish and birds and lions and bugs, began to mold something new; something that would see and know and laugh and love. With the Community's image as a mold and model, a new thing was brought into being.

This new thing would be the pinnacle of everything God had created. The Lord would point out the sunrise and this new thing's breath would catch. When a thunderstorm would pass through, it was God to whom this new thing would come running for protection. The Community of Love would hold this small creature and explain that everything would be okay.

God formed this living being. The Community breathed its own life into this thing. The Community of Father, Son, and Holy Spirit—the relationship that was full, complete, and needed nothing—invited these new, small, frail children to share this powerful community. And it was so very good.

God could have formed the children without the ability to choose their course. That decision had been made with the stars and planets and mountains and streams. None of these had been given the freedom to choose—planets and moons are in their orbit and have no ability to choose to do otherwise. Mountains are tall and strong, but they will never think, "I want to be a valley now." Gravity does not consider whether it will influence objects or not.

This decision allowed the universe to be orderly, but it also ensured that no planet would ever write a song about the Creator. True, God created great beauty in the planet—a beauty that is a song in itself—but it isn't a song that the planet composed.

In humanity, God has created something that is able to create as God creates. Not on the same level; neither as equal nor rival, but as something that understands, as God does, that when love is present beautiful things result.

The People of This Story

We are the people of this Story. We are the rememberers of the Story of God, the Community of Love. Not only this, we *are* the story of the Community of Love in action. This understanding of God teaches us how to receive one another, to speak of salvation, to engage in the mission of God, and even to praise the God who has come near to make community possible.

We bring this identity with us as we approach the text of Scripture. Of course, there may be some individuals in the reading community that do not embrace this identity personally—and their voices have the potential to deeply enrich our experience of reading together. One person may be skeptical of religious belief in general and another may be suspicious of the Judeo-Christian story in particular—possibly due to past experiences with people who *do* claim the Judeo-Christian identity. Others, encountering the story for the first time, have never had reason or opportunity to form any opinion at all.

This book—the Bible—belongs to the community, and while it is best read in community, each of us are invited into the story. The Bible is not hidden away or accessible only to those deemed to be properly initiated. Still, as with any piece of literature, there is a certain sense in which we must approach the text on its own terms to grasp what it is communicating.

Genesis 1–2: The Community of Love

Approaching the Text on Its Own Terms

Several years ago, when my oldest son was in the fourth grade, I was blessed with one of "those moments." Parents, guardians, and any adults who are involved in the life of young children in some way know that, from time to time, a glimpse into the thought processes of a child can be incredibly profound and moving. The astounding nature of these moments is often highlighted by the seemingly mundane context from which they arise.

My son and his classmates were beginning to move beyond *how* a sentence is structured to consider the questions of *why* and *for what purpose*. Working with the genres of "entertainment," "information," and "persuasion," students were asked to identify intentions in a series of sentences.

That afternoon, as I was looking over his schoolwork, I noticed one red "X" by the sentence, "Slavery is evil and should never have been allowed in this country or any other." I couldn't help but smile when I saw he selected *information*, rather than *persuasion*, as the sentence's intention. When I asked why he chose that answer, his response was as reasonable as it was (technically) incorrect.

"Because slavery *is* evil and it should never have been allowed in this country. That isn't something we need to persuade people to believe, it is just a true statement. Why would I need to persuade anyone of that?"

His view of the world, though beautiful, was at odds with the assignment's intention—and, okay, technically it was also at odds with the function of the sentence.

I had to agree with his reasoning, and suggested that we could both continue viewing his answer as correct. However, we then discussed the importance of understanding why it was also incorrect and how to recognize that distinction in future contexts.

In very simplistic terms to respond to a question we need to understand what is and is not being asked, presented, or discussed.

The same counsel applies to each of us as we come to the pages of the Bible. We are invited to bring our own convictions with us to the text, but we need to know that the authors may not have been writing to address those convictions. Just as our community likely includes great diversity in perspective, we will also encounter different purposes and intentions in the various stories we encounter in this text.

That doesn't mean the only wisdom and truth in a passage is found in the author's original intent—my son's homework is a reminder of that. However, just as with that assignment, the impact of the unexpected wisdom is diminished without awareness of what was being said in the first place.

Written to the Community of Faith

For the most part, the Bible is written to the believing community. It is not primarily a document designed to convince skeptics, but rather to strengthen and equip the people of God. That doesn't mean skeptics are unwelcome or that this story isn't compelling enough to bring about a change of perspective. It just means that, most of the time, the concerns of the skeptic were not the authors' primary concern.

So, for instance, very few passages seem interested in providing a case for the existence of God. While existence itself is treated as a given, the significance and implications of that existence are addressed in detail. This makes perfect sense if the intended audience is the believing community. "We believe, what then shall we do with this belief?"

Imagine that your neighbor is unaware the Bible was written to those with a shared belief in the existence of God. However, your neighbor works with an aggressive Christian who uses the Bible as if it were a resource for debating with skeptics. After some personal study, your neighbor might decide that the rhetorical devices used to prove God's existence in this book are laughable and dismiss the whole project.

The travesty here is not that a "potential convert" rejected the message, or dismissed and disrespected the Bible. It is certainly not that this non-Christian won a debate against an evangelistic Christian. What is truly sad is that both have missed experiencing the incredible impact of a story that is largely unconcerned with the very thing they were debating!

Another example, which pertains directly to our passage, is the perceived conflict between the Bible and science. Again, this entire argument is based on a failure to appreciate what the story intends to communicate. It may be hard to imagine, but neither the Bible's authors nor its original recipients had ever heard of Charles Darwin.

This "debate" between evolution and the Bible is ridiculous because the Bible isn't even aware the debate exists. Genesis was not written to give a twenty-first century scientific description of the origin of the cosmos. Coming to these pages for ammunition in our arguments for or against evolution is unproductive and unfair. On the other hand, coming to these pages to ask who this God is, or how this God feels about our world and its inhabitants, well, that is a different story altogether.

In the introduction we discussed how a missional reading of the Bible will take into account the missional direction and purpose of the story, identity of the recipients, and engagement with culture. This is what we mean by reading as the people of this story.

And so, let's turn our attention to the beginning of our story.

Reading the Creation Narratives with a Missional Lens

> In the beginning God created the heavens and the earth. Now the earth was formless and empty, darkness was over the surface of the deep, and the Spirit of God was hovering over the waters.[1]

Genesis, as the name implies, is a story of beginnings. It is significant that the opening words are, "In the beginning God." The story doesn't begin with us—or our ancient predecessors. The action is initiated by God, and the narrative tells us a lot more

---

1. Gen 1:1-2 NIV.

about God than it does about the early days of Earth and the cosmos. This story, like the term *missional*, is first about God.

As we continue to read through this chapter, what stands out the most? Whether this is your first or thousandth time reading it, take a few moments to read the words slowly and pay attention.

> And God said, "Let there be light," and there was light. God saw that the light was good, and he separated the light from the darkness. God called the light "day," and the darkness he called "night." And there was evening, and there was morning—the first day.
>
> And God said, "Let there be a vault between the waters to separate water from water." So God made the vault and separated the water under the vault from the water above it. And it was so. God called the vault "sky." And there was evening, and there was morning—the second day.
>
> And God said, "Let the water under the sky be gathered to one place, and let dry ground appear." And it was so. God called the dry ground "land," and the gathered waters he called "seas." And God saw that it was good.
>
> Then God said, "Let the land produce vegetation: seed-bearing plants and trees on the land that bear fruit with seed in it, according to their various kinds." And it was so. The land produced vegetation: plants bearing seed according to their kinds and trees bearing fruit with seed in it according to their kinds. And God saw that it was good. And there was evening, and there was morning—the third day.
>
> And God said, "Let there be lights in the vault of the sky to separate the day from the night, and let them serve as signs to mark sacred times, and days and years, and let them be lights in the vault of the sky to give light on the earth." And it was so. God made two great lights—the greater light to govern the day and the lesser light to govern the night. He also made the stars. God set them in the vault of the sky to give light on the earth, to govern the day and the night, and to separate light from darkness. And God saw that it was good. And there was evening, and there was morning—the fourth day.

Genesis 1–2: The Community of Love

And God said, "Let the water teem with living creatures, and let birds fly above the earth across the vault of the sky." God created the great creatures of the sea and every living thing with which the water teems and that moves about in it, according to their kinds, and every winged bird according to its kind. And God saw that it was good. God blessed them and said, "Be fruitful and increase in number and fill the water in the seas, and let the birds increase on the earth." And there was evening, and there was morning—the fifth day.

And God said, "Let the land produce living creatures according to their kinds: the livestock, the creatures that move along the ground, and the wild animals, each according to its kind." And it was so. God made the wild animals according to their kinds, the livestock according to their kinds, and all the creatures that move along the ground according to their kinds. And God saw that it was good.

Then God said, "Let us make mankind in our image, in our likeness, so that they may rule over the fish in the sea and the birds in the sky, over the livestock and all the wild animals, and over all the creatures that move along the ground."

So God created mankind in his own image, in the image of God he created them; male and female he created them.

God blessed them and said to them, "Be fruitful and increase in number; fill the earth and subdue it. Rule over the fish in the sea and the birds in the sky and over every living creature that moves on the ground."

Then God said, "I give you every seed-bearing plant on the face of the whole earth and every tree that has fruit with seed in it. They will be yours for food. And to all the beasts of the earth and all the birds in the sky and all the creatures that move along the ground—everything that has the breath of life in it—I give every green plant for food." And it was so.

God saw all that he had made, and it was very good. And there was evening, and there was morning—the sixth day. Thus the heavens and the earth were completed in all their vast array.

By the seventh day God had finished the work he had been doing; so on the seventh day he rested from all his work. Then God blessed the seventh day and made it holy, because on it he rested from all the work of creating that he had done.[2]

When we slow down and notice what is going on around us, amazing realizations and inspiration can come from even the most familiar places. Whether we're talking about Genesis 1, the local grocery store, or a child's homework, we can very easily *not see* what is there, because we think we have already seen what there is to see.

What stands out as you read? Some may notice the increasing complexity of creation as if it were a musical score with a dramatic crescendo building anticipation. Hearing this, another person might describe how the phrase, "and there was evening, and there was morning . . ." adds to the musical feeling and almost feels like a chorus between the verses. Others may have gotten lost in reflection after encountering the words, "And God said, 'Let there be light,' and there was light." What kind of being is this God? Just like that, speaking light into existence as if it were no big deal at all.

Imagine how amazing that would seem to people who had never once flipped a light switch or activated the flashlight app on their iPhone. You can almost hear an audible gasp from the audience as these words were spoken for the first time.

Some of us may have noticed that there is very little similarity between us and God as described in this chapter. We may not be sure who or what this God is yet, but it doesn't seem like we have a lot in common.

It isn't so obvious to us reading in English, but the Spirit of God is hovering over more than water in this story. This was not just the water of some ancient ocean. God is over *the deep* . . . the abyss . . . chaos itself.

---

2. Gen 1:3–31 NIV.

Genesis 1–2: The Community of Love

Humanity is caught up amid the chaos and our lives are often tossed around like tiny boats on this ocean. We all experience this to one degree or another. But this God hovers above it all; removed from the very things that humans strive their entire lives to evade, escape, and conquer.

No, whatever and whoever this God is, we are not very much alike at all.

Whenever someone notices this in the text it tends to bring about two very different reactions from the rest of the group. Some will say, "I don't like that. It seems too impersonal. How can I hope to connect with such a being?"

Others will respond, "No, this is fantastic. Imagine a being even more powerful than chaos; someone (or something) that speaks universes into existence—so much bigger and greater than anything else we know. And even if it doesn't make sense, we are somehow created in the image of this God. We may be different, but we are connected. I like this picture very much."

As I imagine the first recipients hearing these words, I suspect there was a similarly diverse reception. Among people whose lives are filled with peril, instability, and chaos, some look to those who share their experience and others find hope in those who have risen above it all.

But there is more to this beginning, so we should continue reading before drawing too many conclusions, and, again, we should probably take our time, letting these words sink in.

> This is the account of the heavens and the earth when they were created, when the Lord God made the earth and the heavens.
>
> Now no shrub had yet appeared on the earth and no plant had yet sprung up, for the Lord God had not sent rain on the earth and there was no one to work the ground, but streams came up from the earth and watered the whole surface of the ground. Then the Lord God formed a man from the dust of the ground and breathed into his nostrils the breath of life, and the man became a living being.

Now the Lord God had planted a garden in the east, in Eden; and there he put the man he had formed. The Lord God made all kinds of trees grow out of the ground—trees that were pleasing to the eye and good for food. In the middle of the garden were the tree of life and the tree of the knowledge of good and evil.

A river watering the garden flowed from Eden; from there it was separated into four headwaters. The name of the first is the Pishon; it winds through the entire land of Havilah, where there is gold. (The gold of that land is good; aromatic resin and onyx are also there.) The name of the second river is the Gihon; it winds through the entire land of Cush. The name of the third river is the Tigris; it runs along the east side of Ashur. And the fourth river is the Euphrates.

The Lord God took the man and put him in the Garden of Eden to work it and take care of it. And the Lord God commanded the man, "You are free to eat from any tree in the garden; but you must not eat from the tree of the knowledge of good and evil, for when you eat from it you will certainly die."

The Lord God said, "It is not good for the man to be alone. I will make a helper suitable for him."

Now the Lord God had formed out of the ground all the wild animals and all the birds in the sky. He brought them to the man to see what he would name them; and whatever the man called each living creature, that was its name. So the man gave names to all the livestock, the birds in the sky and all the wild animals.

But for Adam no suitable helper was found. So the Lord God caused the man to fall into a deep sleep; and while he was sleeping, he took one of the man's ribs and then closed up the place with flesh. Then the Lord God made a woman from the rib he had taken out of the man, and he brought her to the man.

The man said, "This is now bone of my bones and flesh of my flesh; she shall be called 'woman,' for she was taken out of man." That is why a man leaves his father and mother and is united to his wife, and they become one flesh. Adam and his wife were both naked, and they felt no shame.³

What do you notice as you read through this chapter? What stands out?

Of course, one of the first comments is usually about being naked, and how this may be the best final sentence in a chapter ever. Sometimes, when we're really being honest, we talk about the sense of loss we feel as we consider how different life would be if we could be naked and feel no shame. Most of us consider it a successful day if we can avoid feeling shame in a fully clothed state.

And then it hits us: the Bible's account of creation begins with a description of God hovering above the chaos and concludes with a description humanity standing naked without shame, which seems about as accurate a description of existing above the chaos as any. We may have more in common with this God than we first imagined. And, sadly, the picture of life without shame is often harder to imagine or comprehend than a God who hovers over the deep and calls forth firm foundations.

Is this how we were created to exist—fully exposed without a bit of shame? And if so, why are so many people tortured by shame in the name of God and at the hands of God's people? Feel free to let that one sit in front of your face for a while . . . the next paragraph is content to wait until you're ready.

If this conversation doesn't consume our time together (which it can easily do) one of the next things we notice and discuss might be that God seems more human in this chapter or, at least, now we are able see more of a family resemblance.

Some folks, such as myself, are struck by the imagery of God walking in the garden, kneeling down to scoop up a handful of dust and creating a person, and then physically breathing life into the person. I am captivated by the idea of God being willing to get the divine hands dirty on our account.

Ever since the birth of my children Genesis 2 has consistently reminded me of certain small, quiet moments. Bathing my infant

---

3. Gen 2:4–25 NIV.

sons in the sink, rocking them to sleep, and making up stories about little boys going on great adventures. It makes me think of hiking with them through the state park and carrying the little one for the second half of the journey. These kinds of stories are not cosmic in scope, but they are as deep and formative as the cosmos is vast and majestic.

One Creation Story, or Two?

At this point someone might possibly say, "Wait a minute, didn't God already create people? Didn't God already *speak* people into being? This section begins with the words, 'This is the story of the heavens and the earth when they were created.' That makes it sound like we have two separate creation stories. And they're very different ways of creating. So, what gives?"

And now, we are faced with a choice. We can try to explain away the presence of two different creation accounts—some scholars have done a fairly convincing job of that. We can also simply ignore the possible disparity and move on. There are, of course, those who say, "Aha! This proves that the Bible is just quaint, superstitious, outdated fiction."

These are all possible responses, but they are not the *only* possible responses. Perhaps now it is easier to see why it helps to know the intended audience and purpose of a book. If we function as though we're dealing with twenty-first century questions and answers, then these responses make a lot of sense. Appreciating the kinds of questions this story is addressing has an enormous amount of bearing on figuring out what to do with these first two chapters.

The story of the Bible begins with two brief vignettes that reveal God and God's posture toward creation—two glimpses into the activity of God. We need both and we could benefit from more still. God is indeed the-one-who-is-not-at-all-like-us, the-one-who-is-above-the-chaos, the-one-who-speaks.

God is also the Community of Love who has freely chosen to step into the midst of chaos with us in a move of incredible hospitality and compassion. God is the one who kneels, scoops, breathes, and walks in the garden with creation. When we are in need of hope found in someone who is above the chaos, there is God. When we are in search of one who stands beside us amid the fray, there is God. When we long for someone to believe in us, when we hunger for meaning, and thirst for purpose, we discover that the very same God who speaks universes into being has also spoken blessing and commissioning on humanity.

It isn't just the walking and hands-on forming that sets a different tone in the second chapter of Genesis. Notice the choice of language in verse 8: "Now the Lord God had planted a garden in the East, in Eden."

God . . . *planted a garden*?

You and I plant gardens, but God? Why? Given all the other stuff happening in these opening chapters, it is easy to miss this little word choice. However, I can't help but wonder what a decision to plant a garden—and the inclusion of this language in the story—tells us about God.

It makes sense that the contents of this garden might be helpful in our quest to understand. First, this is where God chose to place the people, so maybe this highlights the intentionality, care, and consideration given to where God and these people will share space.

It also says that the Lord caused all kinds of plants and trees to spring up from the ground. The presence of fruit-bearing trees makes perfect sense given that people would be living there, yet this isn't just about functionality and sustainability because it says these plants were also pleasing to the eye.

Here we find another clue as to why it says God *planted* the garden. Upon hearing or reading the "Community of Love" narrative, people sometimes ask about the examples I use to describe God's intended relationship with the children. "Pointing out sunsets and running to God in thunderstorms are nice images, but how do you know this was God's intention?"

To be clear, I claim no special revelation or insight. I have no way of knowing if sunsets and thunderstorms played any part in the creation of humanity. However, as I read this section about the garden I cannot help but infer these relational aspects. Often our reflection and discussion on the creation narrative seems to rush from "God created" to "God commanded," and then we immediately move on to "Humanity rebelled."

As often as we do this, we do it to our detriment. Slow down. Pay attention. Look around. This place, intended for God and humanity to dwell together, was created specifically as a space of beauty and connection. It was not simply a nice spot that God happened to choose, but was rather a garden that God planted precisely for this purpose. That purpose involved not just food for survival, but also beauty for enjoyment.

However, that isn't all that was in the garden, is it? There was also temptation . . . even danger. Right in the middle of this garden we find reference to two specific trees. In perhaps one of the greatest examples of downplaying ever, the tree of life and the tree of the knowledge of good and evil are mentioned in a completely offhand manner.

"Oh yeah, I almost forgot, there were a couple trees with names in the middle of the garden. So, anyway, there was also . . ."[4] We get several sentences about rivers and gold and aromatic spices, but just one little throwaway sentence about magic trees.

Magic. Trees.

Then God talks with Adam about his new home, points out the great features, and drops a huge bombshell announcement. "See that tree in the middle? Don't eat from it or you'll die."

Isn't it interesting that nothing is mentioned about eating from the tree of life? A tree that grants immortality with no commands to avoid it. Why didn't Adam march straight over and take a bite? Perhaps, as one without knowledge of good and evil, Adam had no fear of death, thus no desire for immortality. We don't know, because there simply isn't very much attention given to this immortality tree in the narrative.

---

4. See Gen 2:9b. Yes, 9b, as in, not even enough commentary to warrant its own verse number.

Genesis 1–2: The Community of Love

There is a command not to eat from the other tree, but no explanation as to why this deadly tree was planted here, in this place, and not in some distant location. Oh, and there is also no mention of *why* there were magical trees in the first place! When we slow down and think about it, Eden seems a lot more like Narnia than Earth.

To make sense of these odd inclusions, we could spend time unpacking the different creation myths and cultural expectations of ancient Mesopotamia. That would certainly be an interesting and beneficial conversation. In fact, that's a really good idea—we should do that. However, for now we'll focus on how the text functions as we have it, what it says about God, and what kind of people it serves to form.

So far, we have learned that God's act of creation was not predicated on some need for worshippers, servants, or underlings. Rather than showing ambivalence or contempt, God has expressed great pleasure in humanity. Furthermore, we've seen that, in the act of creation, God demonstrated hospitality and desire for connection with humanity. However, this same God also placed a source of temptation and danger right in their midst.

This is not a Thomas Kinkaid painting: a quaint, pretty, but completely sterile landscape. The relationship between God and humanity has inherent risk intentionally planted right in the middle of its origin story. In that way, Eden serves as a pretty decent metaphor for life on earth. Beauty and danger growing together from the same soil.

At this point, some of those who know, or think they know, where this story is headed (and perhaps even those who don't) may attempt to steer the conversation to the next chapter. Yes, the warning presented in the creation narrative is foreshadowing. Yes, things are about to go south. Yes, even among those with little to no connection to the Bible, most people are at least somewhat familiar with the story and tragic consequences associated with this particular tree. "The Fall" that Adam and Eve (and by extension, all of humanity) experienced has inspired innumerable sermons, books, doctrines, and even hermeneutics. Yes, we know all about the curse. Or . . . at least we think we do.[5] So, why not formally include the third chapter in our discussion of creation?

Reading the Story in Sequence

Simply put, we do not include Genesis 3 in our discussion of the creation narrative because it is not part of the creation narrative.

That's really the point. It isn't that we're avoiding, dismissing, or devaluing what comes next in this story. We are trying to remember that it comes next—after the creation narrative.

The first two chapters of Genesis tell us about the God who created everything and how that God intends to relate to creation in general and humanity in particular. Based on those descriptions, Genesis 3 then picks up with questions about why things are the way they are now and what God is doing about it.

Practically speaking, the first two chapters of Genesis provide us with the starting point and the interpretive lens through which we read the chapters (and books) that follow.

Unfortunately, many people seem to include Genesis 3 as the climax and main point of the creation narrative, and so allow it to become their interpretive foundation. That mindset creates a very particular hermeneutic. It can easily lead us to see the world (and humanity) as evil, broken, and inherently ungodly. It might even convince us that attempts to view the world and humanity in any other way would be unbiblical.

If Genesis 3 is the beginning of our story we may believe that God merely tolerates humanity, and that our somewhat transactional relationship with this God is tenuously predicated upon upholding a legal contract. Furthermore, we may well develop a perspective of God's holiness based on our own expectations of how lords interact with peasants, bosses with employees, masters with servants. In that case, the mere offer of any contractual

---

5. Some people might be shocked to realize that though "The Fall" is about as well known as any biblical story, the Bible never refers to the events of Genesis 3 in those terms. This descriptive phrase is no more native to the Bible itself than the chapter and verse numbers.

Genesis 1–2: The Community of Love

agreement between us is a surprising, inexplicable, perhaps even scandalous, offer of pardon.

If Genesis 3 is the beginning of our story, we find little room to affirm goodness, beauty, or truth when they are encountered outside of the Judeo-Christian context, because those qualities aren't very important anyway.

If Genesis 3 is the beginning of our story it is easy to dismiss any serious discussions about caring for creation, because creation is simply the cursed ground that humanity must toil over until our salvation is made complete.

If Genesis 3 is the beginning of our story, then we are going to completely miss the *actual* story.

However, when we slow down long enough to read the beginning of our story, we realize that God created the physical universe out of love and with great satisfaction. The world and its inhabitants are beloved! We have not yet discussed Genesis 3 because we started at the beginning, and Genesis 3 is not the beginning.

Our story begins with a proclamation that God is the transcendent creator who exists above the chaos, and also the incredibly hospitable Community of Love who formed us personally. There is no sense of compulsion, obligation or aloof detachment in God's creative act. Our connection to this God is not tenuous or scandalous; it is part of the very essence of our creation.

It is important to know where this story begins, and where it does not begin, because that distinction may change how Christians relate to God, to one another, to non-Christians, and to the rest of creation.

If the Bible starts in Genesis 1, then the story itself disputes the idea that everything in this life is a necessary evil we endure until God destroys it all and sends us to a spiritual realm. We are called to act as agents of co-creation with God. Where there is brokenness, hurt and despair, we are commissioned as partners in the mission of healing and reconciliation.

This world is not a disposable resource to be tossed aside on a whim. Every tree, every rock, every fish, and every bird are a reminder of the God who walks in the garden; of the God who says, "It is good."

Beyond how we view God and treat the planet, the beginning of our story also has profound implications for how we treat other people. In the beginning, humanity was created in the image of God. If people are the image bearers of God, then people—ALL people—are to be treated with dignity and respect.

The image of God is in our created nature! It is not a conditional blessing. We cannot point to what occurs in Genesis 3 as an excuse to hate, abuse, mistreat, or neglect. The connection between God and humanity is already established and its foundation is deep. Nothing can change that.

How we understand the basis of this relationship and the purpose of this story will shape our interactions with just about everything. The good news is Genesis 3 is not the beginning of our story.

And so we have the actual opening narratives, the beginning, the genesis of Genesis. By slowing down and looking we've noticed a lot more than a simple children's story, more than a history lesson and something wholly different from a science textbook.

We have discovered that the main character of this story is God, the one who speaks universes into existence and plants gardens and walks with creatures formed through an up-close-and-personal process.

We noticed that God's first recorded activity is an act of hospitality and invitation into community. It has been immediately apparent that this story will be about a God who values beauty and relationship. This God doesn't remove risk and danger from life, but instead invites creation into a robust adventure and then remains in the middle of the story.

We've found that in this story, humanity is not merely tolerated, but is rejoiced over, blessed, and commissioned to join in the creative adventures in the main character's company.

This is the story of a missionary God, written to people who were created to be on mission with God. With this sort of beginning, what we will discover next?

Genesis 1–2: The Community of Love

Notes from Denise

The first story sets the trajectory. God is a Community of Love. The Community creates because its love is so expansive the Community desires to share that love. The Community speaks, and we are invited into the Story.

And it was good.

It was very good.

And the trajectory is still that the Community calls us, woos us, and desires that we see and share the good, in our time, in our context, in our everyday walk-around lives, inspired by our own experiences and even our own wounds. We can do so knowing that the Community is above the chaos, even while also walking around in the chaos with us.

Can we allow that we will need to struggle to see the way the Community sees, but that in that struggle there is growth and transformation?

What if . . . we really start the story of creation with the creation?

What if . . . we dare to believe we are invited into Community with God right from the beginning?

What if . . . we believe that we are ALL created in the image and likeness of God the Community?

Do we dare?

Are we courageous enough?

3

Who Are We?

Why Things Are the Way Things Are

THE BOOK OF GENESIS ended on a high note. Technically the last verse of Genesis says that Joseph died, was embalmed, and then buried in Egypt . . . but that is not the "high note" to which I'm referring.

Genesis opened with eleven chapters of primeval history—which chronicle the origin stories that informed how the Israelite people understood the world: the origin of the world/creation, of sin, of languages, of Israel and its distinct calling as "God's chosen people," and ancient explanations of enmity with other people groups.

For instance, consider a somewhat jarring story—a tale that certainly seems to be imbued with intentional irony and crude humor, yet is delivered in such a dry, matter-of-fact manner as to leave the reader wondering. The story takes place immediately after the great flood reduced the world's population to one carefully chosen family.

In Genesis 9:20–27, Noah planted a vineyard and drank some of its wine. Then, as one does after drinking too much wine from the vineyard one has planted—or from any vineyard, really—he got drunk, took off all his clothes, and passed out in his tent.

When his son Ham entered the tent and found Noah drunk, naked, and asleep, he immediately went outside to tell his brothers all about it. Apparently, this was not the proper response to this delicate situation,[1] because, when Noah woke up and learned what Ham had done, he was extremely unhappy. Considering the events of the previous night, Noah was probably not in the best mood even before hearing what happened.

The text never specifically names Ham's offensive action. However, it seems to imply, with very little detail, that Ham dishonored his father because after seeing him in this state, he went out to tell his brothers—which, honestly, seems like exactly what most brothers would do in that situation. The honorable action, as demonstrated by those brothers, Shem and Japheth, was, apparently, to enter the tent backwards and, without looking at their father, cover him with a blanket.

Does it seem to anyone else like Noah's furious and long-reaching reaction was perhaps a tiny bit over the top? It is true that Noah was naked and asleep in his own tent, not in the middle of camp. And it is probably also true that Ham should have known it was not proper to run out and make fun of his dad (or whatever it was he was doing). There is a lot we could explore here regarding honor, shame, dignity, and purity in both ancient and contemporary cultures.[2] This story also highlights some important, and timely, questions about authority figures using their position to shift attention and blame onto those whose actions brought their improprieties to light.

These questions may seem irreverent and are perhaps uncomfortable for some to even entertain. However, these are precisely the sorts of things noticed—and commented on—by those who did not grow up reading the Bible, because the text doesn't

---

1. Was there already an established protocol for such a scenario??

2. That conversation extends well beyond our ability to address here. For a more thorough treatment I recommend: deSilva, *Honor, Patronage, Kinship and Purity*.

even try to hide the messiness. Given that there is no attempt in the story to defend Noah's actions, I wonder if this isn't *exactly* how we are expected to respond.

In any case, when Noah learned what transpired, he was furious, and pronounced a curse in response to his son's actions. However, the curse isn't put on Ham, but on Ham's son . . . Canaan.

And there it is.

Why is this strange story included? At least partly, this story is intended to provide backstory, explanation, and justification for Israel conquering, and constantly feuding with, the Canaanites.

We can find these types of stories in every culture. They answer big questions about why things are the way things are, and they do so in ways that orient the members of the community toward one another—and, all too often, away from outsiders.

From Landless Nomad to Egyptian Savior

The remaining chapters of Genesis (chapters 12–50) are referred to as the patriarchal narratives because they are built around the stories of Israel's patriarchs—Abraham, Isaac, and Jacob—and their families. In Genesis 12:1–9 God calls Abram (whose name would later be changed to Abraham), blesses him, and promises him that he will become the father of a great nation. From verse ten to the end of Genesis, the question seems to be, "Will this actually work out?"

The final chapters of Genesis focused not so much on Jacob, but on his favorite son: Joseph. The story is full of dramatic twists and turns: Joseph infuriated his brothers, who thought about killing him, but instead just threw him in a pit and sold him into slavery.[3] Joseph is taken to Egypt where he is sold to Potiphar, Pharaoh's captain of the guard. As a household slave Joseph impressed

---

3. Which is certainly worse than making fun of your naked father, is it not? Joseph's brothers must have been really mad. Have you ever noticed what Joseph's brothers did right after throwing him in a pit? Genesis 37:25 says they sat down to eat their meal. Wow. "Glad that's done. I certainly worked up an appetite. Who's ready for lunch?"

Potiphar and was eventually elevated to the position of attendant, effectively the second-in-command of the entire household.

However, Joseph refused the advances of Potiphar's wife and soon found himself falsely accused of attempted rape and thrown into the king's prison. Ever persistent, while imprisoned Joseph impressed the warden and was placed in charge of the rest of the prisoners. Once again, Joseph had become the second-in-command, this time of the royal prison.

While overseeing the prison, Joseph accurately interpreted the prophetic dreams of two high-profile prisoners—one, the former chief cupbearer, would be restored to his former position, while the other, the former chief baker, would be executed. To the chief cupbearer, he made this request: "But remember me when it is well with you; please do me the kindness to make mention of me to Pharaoh, and so get me out of this place."[4] As we might guess from how this story has progressed, the chief cupbearer was restored but completely forgot about Joseph, who remained imprisoned for two more years. However, eventually Pharaoh had a dream of his own that needed interpretation.

To make a long story short, Joseph became the second-in-command of Egypt.[5]

Not one to hold a grudge, Joseph used his newfound influence not only to save the empire but also to rescue and improve his family's standing.[6]

That is how Genesis ends on a high note: an unbelievable story of Joseph's persistence and God's faithfulness saving the day and making the entire region indebted to the line of Abraham.

Then we turn the page.

---

4. Gen 40:14 NRSV.

5. From despised little brother to arguably the second most powerful person in the world. Well played, Joseph.

6. Though not before having a little fun getting even with his brothers. So, maybe he held a tiny grudge, but I think we can give him that one.

From Savior to Slaves and Back to Nomads

Exodus begins by abruptly taking that high note and tossing it out the window. Over time Joseph was forgotten, and the new Pharaoh decided that there were too many Israelites in Egypt, so they were enslaved. This sets the stage for the well-known story of Moses being called by God to lead the Israelite exodus from Egypt. In the first half of Exodus we read of the burning bush, the ten plagues, the Israelites crossing the Red Sea on dry ground, and Pharaoh's army being drowned by those same waters. It is also where we discover that the people began complaining as soon as they were out of Egypt.

- The people complain, and God provides water.[7]
- The people complain, and God provides quail and manna.[8]
- The people complain and fight with Moses, and God provides water.[9]
- The people are attacked by, and are victorious against, the Amalekites.[10]
- *Then* the people agree to obey, live in covenant with, and be the holy people of God.[11]

God responds graciously and compassionately to the people's complaints in these chapters. Those same complaints elicit a much different reaction later in the story, once the covenant is established and Israel has had an opportunity to "get to know God" a little better.[12]

The people who left Egypt had never read Genesis—which is not surprising, since it had not yet been written. They didn't know much about the God of Moses—the God of their ancestors,

---

7. Exod 15:22–25.
8. Exod 16:1–8.
9. Exod 17:1–7.
10. Exod 17:8–16.
11. Exod 19:1–15, especially 3–8.
12. See Num 11–14 and 20–21.

Abraham, Isaac, and Jacob—or what it meant to be a chosen people. The descendants of Israel's[13] children had been slaves in Egypt for a very long time, during which they did not seem to have the sense of identity and purpose we read about in Genesis.

From No People to God's People

And that is how these people—the newly emancipated, fledgling nation of Israel—found themselves camped out in the desert, discovering their new identity, receiving instructions on how to organize their society and how to live in relationship with this strange God. In that desert (literally and metaphorically) Israel not only became God's people, but also began the long process of setting aside the debilitating and pernicious mindsets accumulated over generations living as "no people" in slavery to Pharaoh.

For the casual observer, Exodus 25 through 31 may not seem like the most interesting reading material. Chapter after chapter, page after tedious page, of instruction on how to build and use the tabernacle—a giant tent that would function as a mobile temple. However, for an unsettled community, these are more than just construction plans and random rules.

The tabernacle, or tent of meeting, would be where the people gathered for worship, and it would be a center point for the community—regardless of how often they moved about, the people would set up their camp with this Sanctuary in the very center of their community. The tabernacle would also be the place to which the people would look to be reminded that the presence of God was with them, right in their midst.

There were lots of gods in this region and every one of them had a temple. Temples were important because they provided a place for the god to dwell and receive worship. To go to a temple and worship a god was good for you because it was good for the

---

13. In case you missed it, in Genesis 32:22–32, following an evening spent wrestling (literally) with God, Jacob was renamed Israel. That name, which probably means "he struggles with God," is a pretty appropriate name for Jacob . . . and for the Israelites.

god. It was considered a great risk to travel too far away from your god's temple, because a god's power was usually restricted to the region where their temple rested.

This thinking is possibly behind Abram (Abraham) lying to Pharaoh in Genesis 12:10–20. After he arrived in Canaan (where God had sent him), Abraham and his household left and traveled to Egypt because there was a great famine in Canaan. Once in Egypt, he told Sarai (Sarah) to lie about who she was, saying she was his sister rather than his wife. Apparently, Abraham was afraid that because Sarah was beautiful, the Egyptians would kill him and take her for themselves. On the other hand, if they believed she was merely his sister, the Egyptians would not be tempted to commit something as deplorable as murdering Abraham just because they wanted to abduct and enslave Sarah.[14]

Perhaps Abraham was afraid God wouldn't have power to protect them in Egypt because this wasn't God's region. However, this experienced illustrated that, unlike the other gods of the ancient Near East, God is not a regional god. As we might expect, Pharaoh failed to appreciate being the one to provide Abraham clarification on this important aspect about Abraham's own God.[15] Even so, given that this God was on the move and not restricted to one region, the decision to construct a mobile sanctuary—a tabernacle—was certainly appropriate.

The Tabernacle, the Cosmos, and the Garden

It is also significant that the tent of meeting—the place where God's Presence came down and dwelt with the people in a tangible way—was positioned among the people rather than high above and separated from the city. Up to this point in the Exodus story, the Israelites had witnessed the power of God over Egypt and even over creation itself. Just as we saw in the Genesis 1 creation account, these people had witnessed the cosmic aspects of God.

---

14. How noble.

15. Sadly, and disturbingly, we do not get to hear Sarah's opinion on the whole matter.

Who Are We?

However, having read Genesis 2, we know God is more than just an unfathomable cosmic power. And, having read the patriarchal narratives from Genesis 12 through 50, we know that God intends a more intimate connection with Israel.

After all, this is the God who called an elderly couple to start a vibrant new nation; the God whose vibrant new nation was not the superpower Egypt, Assyria, Babylon, or even Philistia—a somewhat small, but powerful nation, known for its fierce warriors. This is the God who listens to slaves and the poor, the God who used an annoying younger brother to save countless people's lives, and a God who settled among a complaining people.

With the construction of the tabernacle, Israel has a visible reminder that God has come near to dwell with them in a new way. The Presence of God is now "ongoing rather than occasional; close, not distant; on-the-move, not fixed . . . No longer are the people—or their mediator—asked to come up to God; God 'comes down' to them. No more trips up the mountain for Moses!"[16] God's interaction with humanity happens on God's terms and often amid the common experiences of normal life. The interaction is holy and sacred because God is present, not because it occurs in an opulent palace. The tabernacle was more than a structure; it carried incredible theological significance.

With that understanding in mind, we are better able to notice the significance of *how* the seemingly boring instructions about the tabernacle are arranged. Chapters 25 through 31 consist of seven distinct speeches,[17] with the final speech issuing a command about the Sabbath as a reminder of the seventh day of creation—the day God rested. The description of the tabernacle is tied to the creation of the world—a microcosm of the whole cosmos.

Much like the effect of Genesis 1 and 2, the tabernacle served as both cosmic and intimate reminder. As with the garden of Eden before it, the tabernacle was a place of intimate connection between God and people.

---

16. Birch et al., *Theological Introduction*, 133, 135.
17. The seven speeches begin in: 25:1; 30:11, 17, 22, 34; 31:1, 12.

> I will put my dwelling place among you, and I will not abhor you. I will walk among you and be your God, and you will be my people. I am the Lord your God, who brought you out of Egypt so that you would no longer be slaves to the Egyptians; I broke the bars of your yoke and enabled you to walk with heads held high.[18]

This is not the last time we will see this sort of statement regarding God dwelling among the people in such a way. If we fast-forward to the New Testament, John says, "The Word [Jesus] became flesh and made his dwelling among us."[19] And when the Bible proclaims a new, or renewed, heaven and earth in Revelation 21, it says, "Look! God's dwelling place is now among the people, and he will dwell with them. They will be his people, and God himself will be with them and be their God."[20]

The Hebrew word translated "dwell" in Leviticus 26:11 and the Greek word translated "dwell/dwelling" in John 1:14 and Revelation 21:3 are forms of the word for tabernacle or tent. From beginning to end, the Bible shows us that God consistently draws near and dwells among us.

God walked with Adam and Eve in the garden, God dwelled and moved about in the desert with Israel, God dwelled and walked among us in first century Jerusalem, and God will dwell among the cities when heaven and earth are renewed. The tabernacle was more than a temporary dwelling place, it was symbolic of how God consistently chose to draw near and dwell among the people.

Which makes King David's desire to build a temple very interesting.

> After the king was settled in his palace and the Lord had given him rest from all his enemies around him, he said to Nathan the prophet, "Here I am, living in a house of cedar, while the ark of God remains in a tent."
>
> Nathan replied to the king, "Whatever you have in mind, go ahead and do it, for the Lord is with you."

---

18. Lev 26:11–13 NIV.
19. John 1:14 NIV.
20. Rev 21:3 NIV.

> But that night the word of the Lord came to Nathan, saying:
>
> "Go and tell my servant David, 'This is what the Lord says: Are you the one to build me a house to dwell in? I have not dwelt in a house from the day I brought the Israelites up out of Egypt to this day. I have been moving from place to place with a tent as my dwelling. Wherever I have moved with all the Israelites, did I ever say to any of their rulers whom I commanded to shepherd my people Israel, "Why have you not built me a house of cedar?"'[21]

At first glance, David's declaration seems reasonable enough. The king shouldn't have a palace that outshines the Lord's temple—or the Lord's tent! That has a certain logic to it. However, Nathan's initial response, and most assuredly the message Nathan later receives from God, raises some important issues. David simply decided God needed a temple—apparently, the Lord didn't need to have any input.

Except that, requested or not, God had some input to share.

It is interesting that David assumed God needed an elaborate temple because David had an elaborate palace. This is an ironic and troubling realization given the origin of Israelite kings, and, especially, the story of King David's rise to power.

When the people of Israel first began clamoring for a king, God stated plainly that they were rejecting God with this request. Not only that, but they did not understand what they were asking. Kings build empires; it's what they do. The people pay for that empire—financially, physically, and emotionally—it's what they do. God warned the people that Israel's kings would be no different.

None of this mattered to the people because they wanted to be "like all the other nations."[22] That is an interesting motivation given that Israel was intended to be distinct from the other nations.

Do you know what else "all the other nations" had? Temples.

---

21. 2 Sam 7:1–7 NIV.
22. 1 Sam 8:20 NIV.

David should have been the first to question whether God would have any interest in an impressive temple. If God were interested in such showy displays, David would never have been king. In fact, after rejecting King Saul, God passed over each of David's older, more impressive brothers, saying, "Do not consider his appearance or his height, for I have rejected him. The Lord does not look at the things people look at. People look at the outward appearance, but the Lord looks at the heart."[23]

Furthermore, God already had an impressive temple: "Heaven is my throne, and the earth is my footstool. Where is the house you will build for me?"[24]

God never requested a temple. God does not even need a temple, because the whole of creation serves that purpose—how does one expect to build something to improve on the entire cosmos?

> Now then, tell my servant David, "This is what the Lord Almighty says: I took you from the pasture, from tending the flock, and appointed you ruler over my people Israel. I have been with you wherever you have gone, and I have cut off all your enemies from before you. Now I will make your name great, like the names of the greatest men on earth. And I will provide a place for my people Israel and will plant them so that they can have a home of their own and no longer be disturbed. Wicked people will not oppress them anymore, as they did at the beginning and have done ever since the time I appointed leaders over my people Israel. I will also give you rest from all your enemies.
>
> The Lord declares to you that the Lord himself will establish a house for you: When your days are over and you rest with your ancestors, I will raise up your offspring to succeed you, your own flesh and blood, and I will establish his kingdom. He is the one who will build a house for my Name, and I will establish the throne of his kingdom forever. I will be his father, and he will be my son. When he does wrong, I will punish him with a

---

23. 1 Sam 16:7 NIV.
24. Isa 66:1 NIV.

rod wielded by men, with floggings inflicted by human hands. But my love will never be taken away from him, as I took it away from Saul, whom I removed from before you. Your house and your kingdom will endure forever before me; your throne will be established forever."[25]

The depth of the king's presumptuousness becomes extremely clear when contrasted with God's humbling response and counter-offer. As it turns out, while God does not need help building a house, David certainly does.

Though David will not be the one to build the temple, the events leading to its construction have now been set in motion. Israel has begun the transition from being a tabernacle people to a Temple people. That transition will lead to a period of relative stability, prosperity, and political influence. And yet, this transition will also set Israel down the path toward destruction and exile. That is precisely the situation we will encounter as we turn our attention toward the book of Isaiah.

Notes from Denise

Clearly, God is on the move all through the Story. As God's people, we choose to move *with* the Community, or *away from* the Community. God dwells among his people. We may choose to dwell with God, or we may choose to build a Temple and try to keep the Community inside.

From a God who moves and dwells with us, we attempt to create a monument that does not.

From a God who wants to make us a set-apart people, we instead choose what seems a safer path to "be like all the other nations."

What if... we choose instead to leave the Temple doors open and stop trying to keep the Community contained in a nice, tidy place?

What if... we focus on the moving and dwelling instead?

---

25. 2 Sam 7:8–16 NIV.

4

Isaiah 56–59: Who Will We Become?

I SAT PERCHED ON a rock at Little Round Top, in Gettysburg, Pennsylvania—the somber and solitary bronze statue of G. K. Warren just above and behind me, a valley of indescribable beauty and unimaginable tragedy spread out before me.

Just below and to the left was the area of treacherously strewn boulders aptly named Devil's Den. Gazing down on that spot, I could believe every single story about those rocks being haunted by the ghosts of the soldiers who died in their midst.

Across the field was Seminary Ridge where the main concentration of confederate troops and artillery struck fear into the people of Gettysburg. To my right, I could see sections of Cemetery Ridge—the "high water mark of the Confederacy." That was the point at which Robert E. Lee's troops were turned back on the third day of fighting—and it was the closest they ever came to moving on Washington, DC.

There, on that hilltop, surrounded by the oddly peaceful clamor of cicadas, I gazed across fields, creeks, ridges, tree lines, and staging points of atrocity and horror; places where thousands upon thousands of lives were lost over the span of three days in July 1863.

And then, in the waning light of day, the sound of cicadas was replaced by the crystal-clear notes from an old veteran's bugle, as the lonely sounds of Taps echoed across the valley.

Isaiah 56–59: Who Will We Become?

Already overwhelmed by the experience, I was brought to tears by the audacious beauty of the sunset over Gettysburg. I felt, more than understood, the truth of the words "hallowed ground," and knew with every fiber of my being that I had entered a Thin Place. I was unable to speak, unable to move, very nearly unable to breathe as I was struck by the incongruence of the moment. How was such transcendent beauty still possible in a place so marred by violence and loss?

I wondered how the hills could stand tall under the weight of such memory. The hills, refusing to respond, remained standing.

I wondered how the winds could still glide across a valley that had been drenched by the blood and tears of so many. The winds, indifferent to my questions, continued on their way.

I wondered how the trees and plants found the will to continue blooming year after year. The trees and plants, showing no sign of duress, continued their imperceptible but utterly predictable progress toward autumn.

Well before dawn the next morning, I made my way along Seminary Ridge—on the Western edge of the battlefield, across from Little Round Top. I walked out into the dew-covered grass, past the towering figure of Robert E. Lee and the Virginia Monument, and sat on a bench to watch the sunrise.

In the light of that new day, I looked out across the long stretch of open field up to Cemetery Ridge where, on July 3, 1863, the Union defenses repelled Pickett's charge. The horrific exchange was over in less than an hour, resulting in around 7,500 casualties, and effectively ending the battle of Gettysburg.

In the Celtic tradition, it is said that heaven and earth are only three feet apart, but in a Thin Place that distance is even less. When we enter such a place, barriers become translucent and the neatly compartmentalized segments of our lives refuse to stay tucked away.

Personally, I suspect a Thin Place is not so much a location where the boundary between heaven and earth is closer, but rather a place where—for whatever reason—we are more aware of their immediacy: an experience of time and space where the boundaries we typically perceive are revealed as illusion.

WHAT KIND OF GOD?

Sitting alone in that open field, I was bombarded by the complexity of sorrow and joy, guilt and peace, wonder and despair. Over the course of an evening and a morning I attempted to notice and experience what was around me without trying to understand, explain, analyze, or unpack. (My friends and family will likely have noticed and recognize the significance of the word "attempted.")

Many of the thoughts and emotions I encountered in that place were fueled by my connection to the history of Gettysburg and the American Civil War. On that hill, I wrestled with questions about myself in relation to that history. I couldn't help but wonder,[1] as someone born and raised in Texas and deeply committed to the dignity and shared humanity of all people, where would I have stood on this battlefield?

One after another, like waves endlessly crashing into a rocky shore, the thoughts and emotions rushed over me:

... Sorrow over the loss of life.

... Lament for the tragedy and violence of war.

... Anger at the injustices that made this war all but inevitable.

... Peace and contentment in the presence of nature's simple beauty.

... Excitement to finally see this place with my own eyes.

... Joy in being able to share this important experience with my three sons.

... Guilt and confusion at feeling peace, excitement, and joy amidst so many reminders of sorrow and pain.

Though I can never know to what degree, I have no doubt the emotional impact of this, my first visit to Gettysburg, was influenced by the timing of our trip. I stood on Little Round Top exactly one week after the July 7, 2016, shooting in Dallas, when a lone gunman shot two civilians and fourteen police officers, killing five of the officers. The attack took place at an otherwise peaceful Black Lives Matter protest that, like several others across the country, had been organized after Alton Sterling was shot and killed by

---

1. In this context, "wonder" serves as shorthand for "agonize on a precipice of doubt, shame, and self-loathing."

police in Louisiana on July 5 and Philando Castille was shot and killed by police in Minnesota on July 6.

The man who committed this terrible act, Micah Johnson, was not associated with the Black Lives Matter movement or the protest. Dallas Police Chief David Brown stated, "[Johnson] said he was upset about the recent police shootings. The suspect said he was upset at white people. The suspect stated he wanted to kill white people, especially white officers."[2]

Sitting on the edges of that historic field, I was struck by the connection and shared context between three days in July 1863 and three days in July 2016.

I was struck by the connection and shared context with the deaths of Trayvon Martin, Eric Garner, John Crawford III, Michael Brown, Tamir Rice, Eric Harris, Walter Scott, Freddie Gray, Sandra Bland, and too many others.

I was struck by the connection and shared context with the March and November 2009 shooting deaths of four police officers in California and four police officers in Washington, respectively.

I was struck by the connection and shared context with so many people—mostly children—that have been killed in a mass murder or attempted mass murder in U.S. schools since the school shooting in Columbine, Colorado (141 people as of February 2016).[3]

I was struck by the connection and shared context with the nearly countless deaths and senseless acts of violence that take place every day in this country and around the world. Acts of violence that result from fear and greed and desperation. Acts of violence so commonplace they become white noise; just another statistic that our minds cannot, or will not, process and comprehend. For many of us, it is simply easier to ignore, explain away, or shake our heads and retreat with a noble proclamation of "fasting from negativity."

---

2. Fernandez, Pérez-Peña, and Bromwich, "Five Dallas Officers."

3. According to FBI records as reported by ABC News. See Pearle, "School Shootings."

These avoidance strategies may even seem to work for us; that is, until the statistic has a name we know, a face we recognize, or a story we share. Perhaps they work until we find ourselves in a Thin Place, unable to hide behind illusions of separation.

Before leaving the battlefield that first night, my family and I stopped at the cemetery where Abraham Lincoln gave one of the most famous speeches in American history. As I read the Gettysburg Address to my sons, history intruded on the present and called us to remember.

> Four score and seven years ago our fathers brought forth on this continent, a new nation, conceived in Liberty, and dedicated to the proposition that all men are created equal.
>
> Now we are engaged in a great civil war, testing whether that nation, or any nation so conceived and so dedicated, can long endure. We are met on a great battlefield of that war. We have come to dedicate a portion of that field, as a final resting place for those who here gave their lives that that nation might live. It is altogether fitting and proper that we should do this.
>
> But, in a larger sense, we cannot dedicate—we cannot consecrate—we cannot hallow—this ground. The brave men, living and dead, who struggled here, have consecrated it, far above our poor power to add or detract. The world will little note, nor long remember what we say here, but it can never forget what they did here. It is for us the living, rather, to be dedicated here to the unfinished work which they who fought here have thus far so nobly advanced. It is rather for us to be here dedicated to the great task remaining before us—that from these honored dead we take increased devotion to that cause for which they gave the last full measure of devotion—that we here highly resolve that these dead shall not have died in vain—that this nation, under God, shall have a new birth of freedom—and that government of the people, by the people, for the people, shall not perish from the earth.
>
> —Abraham Lincoln, November 19, 1863[4]

4. Lincoln, "Gettysburg Address."

It was hard not to hear a tone of accusation and disappointment in Lincoln's words. Have we, the living, truly remained dedicated to this unfinished work? What justification can we provide for the work remaining so noticeably and painfully unfinished after so many years?

I believe in the importance of faith, hope, and love—especially in moments of despair. I recognize the importance of choosing to be the change I want to see. I realize the need to focus on those places where good is being done, can be done, and must be continued. I believe that God is always out ahead of us, working toward reconciliation, restoration, and resurrection. I'm not advocating naïve, head-in-the-sand, "everything will be okay" avoidance of the situation. This is more of a conscious act of defiance, of resistance, of rebellion.

However, these convictions did little to assuage my lament, my frustration, or my confusion on that battlefield. How does one reconcile a sense of loss with a sense of wonder? A sense of despair at the still unfinished work, with a sense of hope in the progress that has been made?

I would not disregard or dishonor the sacrifices offered, the victories won, or the progress made by those who have fought and continue to fight for the proposition that all people are created equal. Neither would I cheapen those sacrifices by pretending that the victories and progress have already completed this work.

Returning Home

"This is what the Lord says: Maintain justice and do what is right, for my salvation is close at hand and my righteousness will soon be revealed."[5]

Fifty years had passed since King Nebuchadnezzar sacked Jerusalem, leveled Solomon's Temple, and carried many of the Israelites into exile in Babylon. Those who returned decades later discovered the once great city of Jerusalem in ruins.

---

5. Isa 56:1 NIV.

WHAT KIND OF GOD?

Though this was the first time many of the exiles had seen their homeland, every one of them knew the stories. They had heard of the enormous and seemingly impenetrable city walls. They knew of the broad gates that had granted safe passage to the common folk and priests of Israel as well as to foreign kings, queens, and dignitaries who traveled tremendous distances to see this great marvel for themselves.

Even those born in Babylon carried memories of how the incomparable Solomon's Temple had stood on the hill overlooking the city. Each could recite stories of singing the Psalms of Ascent as family members made the trip together up the mountain to the temple.

Men, women, and children alike knew the dread of seeing enemy soldiers camped outside the gates; the panic of seeing the enemies storm through those gates. They felt the terror of watching as friends and family fell to the sword. They carried the permanent mental image of smoke rising in the distance as thousands of captives made their way into exile.

As one who was coming home, it didn't matter if you had ever physically stood in the city, because you had been there countless times in the memories passed on by your community. And you had likely joined your people as they sat down by the rivers of Babylon and wept for what was lost.

Now, after a lifetime of waiting, you were walking on the same ground where David and Solomon had walked—maybe even the very spot where their feet once stood. You saw landmarks you immediately recognized from the stories. You felt you could almost reach out and touch the sense of rightness and belonging in the air. You were finally home.

And yet.

The walls, the city, the temple . . . all gone. You were back, but you were not. You may have returned, but it was all still just a memory. You were standing in Jerusalem, but the Jerusalem you dreamed of was no more.

The process of rebuilding would involve much more than raising walls, for the buildings were not the only things lying in ruins. The social and political structures had to be reestablished. Would the faith and covenant identity of the people be reaffirmed? Redefined? Replaced altogether?

Rebuilding Jerusalem required an answer to the deceptively elusive question, "Who are we?"

This is the situation and these are the questions addressed in the final chapters of Isaiah.

Major Prophet, Minority Voice

The book of Isaiah is classified as one of the three books of the major prophets, along with Jeremiah and Ezekiel. This classification distinguishes them from the minor prophets—the last twelve books in the Old Testament: Hosea, Joel, Amos, Obadiah, Jonah, Micah, Nahum, Habakkuk, Zephaniah, Haggai, Zechariah, and Malachi.

Side note: the terms "major" and "minor" don't refer to the prophets' relative importance, but rather to the length of the books themselves. In the Hebrew Bible, the twelve minor prophets are included in one book referred to as "The Book of the Twelve" or "The Twelve."

Like all the prophetic books, Isaiah consists of a series of oracles. We can think of these as sermons, speeches, and poems that were later compiled and edited into a single larger document. That is one reason that the prophets (especially the longer, major prophets) can at times seem to jump around in confusing ways.

The potential disorientation gets compounded even more in Isaiah because there was a pretty significant length of time between the first and the last of those speeches—assuming one considers a couple hundred years a significant length of time. And, not to spoil the surprise, no, there wasn't a two hundred-year-old prophet throwing a party in the ruins of Jerusalem to celebrate the completion of his long-awaited manuscript.

Most scholars agree that Isaiah is divided into three segments, each of which corresponds to a distinct period:

- Chapters 1–39: written prior to the fall of Jerusalem (between 742–701 BCE); presents the impending destruction of Jerusalem as God's judgment.

- Chapters 40–55: written during the exile (around 540 BCE); Jerusalem, as a stand-in for the Israelites, is addressed and reassured in captivity.

- Chapters 56–66: written sometime after the exile (between 520–444 BCE); focuses on shaping the Jerusalem to come.[6]

This final section of Isaiah, beginning in chapter 56, can be considered something of a minority voice among the post-exilic writings of Israel/Judah.

Not all the Israelites had been taken into captivity in Babylon. Likewise, not everyone who resided in and around Jerusalem was ethnically or religiously affiliated with Israel/Judah. When questions arose as to the identity of the "true Israelites," many of those who returned from Babylon felt that having participated in the exile was a definitive characteristic of this identity.

This perspective, with both its theological and political ramifications, is represented in books such as Ezra, Haggai, and Zechariah. The emphasis on those who had lived through exile in Babylon (many of whom represented wealthy, influential families), naturally served to devalue, and often fully exclude, those who didn't fit the narrow definition of "us."[7]

Isaiah 56–66, on the other hand, takes a different view with very different implications. Keeping the context in mind, let's look at the first eight verses of chapter 56:

> This is what the Lord says:
> "Maintain justice
> and do what is right,
> for my salvation is close at hand
> and my righteousness will soon be revealed.

---

6. If you're interested, one of my favorite commentaries on Isaiah is the two-volume set by Walter Brueggemann, *Isaiah 1–39* and *Isaiah 40–66*.

7. See Birch et al., *Theological Introduction*, 420–21.

Isaiah 56–59: Who Will We Become?

Blessed is the one who does this—
the person who holds it fast,
who keeps the Sabbath without desecrating it,
and keeps their hands from doing any evil."
Let no foreigner who is bound to the Lord say,
"The Lord will surely exclude me from his people."
And let no eunuch complain,
"I am only a dry tree."
For this is what the Lord says:
"To the eunuchs who keep my Sabbaths,
who choose what pleases me
and hold fast to my covenant—
to them I will give within my temple and its walls
a memorial and a name
better than sons and daughters;
I will give them an everlasting name
that will endure forever.
And foreigners who bind themselves to the Lord
to minister to him,
to love the name of the Lord,
and to be his servants,
all who keep the Sabbath without desecrating it
and who hold fast to my covenant—
these I will bring to my holy mountain
and give them joy in my house of prayer.
Their burnt offerings and sacrifices
will be accepted on my altar;
for my house will be called
a house of prayer for all nations."
The Sovereign Lord declares—
he who gathers the exiles of Israel:
"I will gather still others to them
besides those already gathered."[8]

---

8. Isa 56:1–8 NIV.

WHAT KIND OF GOD?

For Isaiah, the response to the question, "Who are the true Israelites," begins by rejecting exclusion and offering a message of hope, inclusion, and compassion for the marginalized. The two specific groups mentioned here, immigrants and eunuchs, had been marginalized throughout much of Israel's history, and it certainly seems that both continued to anticipate rejection and exclusion. Some voices, such as the voice represented in the book of Ezra, suggested Israel could only be restored through a strict, isolationist purity—perhaps even ethnic cleansing.[9] In contrast, the message from Isaiah is that God, and Israel by extension, resists exclusion and welcomes marginalized people.

Eunuchs, those born outside of a legitimate marriage, and some foreign people would have previously been excluded from the community.[10] Unlike other excluded groups though, eunuchs were particularly vulnerable because they were largely cut off from family—and certainly from offspring who could carry on their name and legacy. Yet, here, God offers not only acceptance, but family and an "enduring name that won't be removed."

Commenting on this passage, Walter Brueggemann states, "The community of Judaism is to be a community that remembers, cherishes, and preserves the name and identity of those otherwise nullified in an uncaring world."[11] To the immigrants, God offers not only inclusion, but *full* inclusion—welcoming their participation in prayer and the sacrificial worship of Israel. God's house is

---

9. The tension between those who returned from exile in Babylon is present throughout the book of Ezra. See chapters 9–10 for Ezra's solution: exiling all who were not pure ethnic Israelites—including wives, children, and grandchildren. This extreme measure was based solely on bloodline, without regard to faith or observance of the Law.

10. Deut 23:1–4 NRSV. "No one whose testicles are crushed or whose penis is cut off shall be admitted to the assembly of the Lord. Those born of an illicit union shall not be admitted to the assembly of the Lord. Even to the tenth generation, none of their descendants shall be admitted to the assembly of the Lord. No Ammonite or Moabite shall be admitted to the assembly of the Lord. Even to the tenth generation, none of their descendants shall be admitted to the assembly of the Lord, because they did not meet you with food and water on your journey out of Egypt, and because they hired against you Balaam son of Beor, from Pethor of Mesopotamia, to curse you."

11. Brueggemann, *Isaiah*, 2:171.

intended to be a house of prayer for all nations. The identity of God's people cannot be separated from their willingness to receive, welcome, and include these marginalized people.

Perhaps we should allow that to sink in for a moment...

After establishing inclusion as a principle aspect of "who we are," Isaiah offers a series of denouncements against corrupt rulers (56:9-12) and the futility of idolatry (57:1-13). These are followed by a promise that, even amid these judgements, God is working towards healing and reconciliation.

Let's pause to read through Isaiah 57:14-21.

> And it will be said:
> "Build up, build up, prepare the road!
> Remove the obstacles out of the way of my people."
> For this is what the high and exalted One says—
> he who lives forever, whose name is holy:
> "I live in a high and holy place,
> but also with the one who is contrite and lowly in spirit,
> to revive the spirit of the lowly
> and to revive the heart of the contrite.
> I will not accuse them forever,
> nor will I always be angry,
> for then they would faint away because of me—
> the very people I have created.
> I was enraged by their sinful greed;
> I punished them, and hid my face in anger,
> yet they kept on in their willful ways.
> I have seen their ways, but I will heal them;
> I will guide them and restore comfort to Israel's mourners,
> creating praise on their lips.
> Peace, peace, to those far and near,"
> says the Lord. "And I will heal them."
> But the wicked are like the tossing sea,
> which cannot rest,
> whose waves cast up mire and mud.
> "There is no peace," says my God, "for the wicked."[12]

---

12. Isa 57:14-21 NIV.

WHAT KIND OF GOD?

As we have already seen in Genesis—and as we'll later discover in the Gospel of John and Revelation—God is not some distant judge lacking connection to or compassion for humanity. God is the one who comes near—the one who lives both, "on high, in holiness, and also with the crushed and the lowly." This is the God who spoke the universe into being, yet walked in the garden with humanity; the one who chose to set up a tent (tabernacle) and dwell among the people. This is *who God is*.

Isaiah then circles back to the issue of reclaiming and restoring Israel's community identity in chapter 58. Perhaps this passage is familiar to you. If so, I encourage you to slow down, pay attention, and listen deeply. And whether it is familiar or not, try to read through the eyes of those wondering what kind of people they would become.

Isaiah 58:1–14 says:

> Shout out, do not hold back!
> Lift up your voice like a trumpet!
> Announce to my people their rebellion,
> to the house of Jacob their sins.
> Yet day after day they seek me
> and delight to know my ways,
> as if they were a nation that practiced righteousness
> and did not forsake the ordinance of their God;
> they ask of me righteous judgments,
> they delight to draw near to God.
> "Why do we fast, but you do not see?
> Why humble ourselves, but you do not notice?"
> Look, you serve your own interest on your fast day,
> and oppress all your workers.
> Look, you fast only to quarrel and to fight
> and to strike with a wicked fist.
> Such fasting as you do today
> will not make your voice heard on high.
> Is such the fast that I choose,
> a day to humble oneself?

Isaiah 56–59: Who Will We Become?

Is it to bow down the head like a bulrush,
and to lie in sackcloth and ashes?
Will you call this a fast,
a day acceptable to the Lord?
Is not this the fast that I choose:
to loose the bonds of injustice,
to undo the thongs of the yoke,
to let the oppressed go free,
and to break every yoke?
Is it not to share your bread with the hungry,
and bring the homeless poor into your house;
when you see the naked, to cover them,
and not to hide yourself from your own kin?
Then your light shall break forth like the dawn,
and your healing shall spring up quickly;
your vindicator shall go before you,
the glory of the Lord shall be your rear guard.
Then you shall call, and the Lord will answer;
you shall cry for help, and he will say, Here I am.
If you remove the yoke from among you,
the pointing of the finger, the speaking of evil,
if you offer your food to the hungry
and satisfy the needs of the afflicted,
then your light shall rise in the darkness
and your gloom be like the noonday.
The Lord will guide you continually,
and satisfy your needs in parched places,
and make your bones strong;
and you shall be like a watered garden,
like a spring of water,
whose waters never fail.
Your ancient ruins shall be rebuilt;
you shall raise up the foundations of many generations;
you shall be called the repairer of the breach,

> the restorer of streets to live in.
> If you refrain from trampling the sabbath,
> from pursuing your own interests on my holy day;
> if you call the sabbath a delight
> and the holy day of the Lord honorable;
> if you honor it, not going your own ways,
> serving your own interests, or pursuing your own affairs;
> then you shall take delight in the Lord,
> and I will make you ride upon the heights of the earth;
> I will feed you with the heritage of your ancestor Jacob,
> for the mouth of the Lord has spoken.[13]

Compassion, concern for others, and actively working for justice are presented here as precursors to the "ancient ruins" being rebuilt. When we consider this alongside the message of chapter 56, we discover a clear call for the social structure of Jerusalem and the identity of God's people to transcend legalistic observance of rules and religious duties. It isn't that rules and religious duties are themselves rejected, but rather they are shown to be inadequate as the defining marks of identity or moral status. "The God of Judaism is not a God who likes to be flattered in a more or less passive routine of worship; this God is out working in the neighborhood and wants all adherents doing the same."[14]

So then, what does it mean when compassion, concern for others, and the pursuit of justice are noticeably absent in our community? In the opening verses of chapter 58, the people are confused as to why God seems to be ignoring their requests for justice. "Why do we fast, but you do not see? Why humble ourselves, but you do not notice?"[15] And yet, the response was not about God's silence, but the people's hypocrisy. The question, in effect, is turned around; Why do you fast and afflict yourself proclaiming your desire for justice if you have no intention of pursuing justice?

The confrontation becomes even more pointed in chapter 59:

---

13. Isa 58:1–14 NRSV.
14. Brueggemann, *Isaiah*, 2:189.
15. Isa 58:3 NRSV.

Isaiah 56–59: Who Will We Become?

> See, the Lord's hand is not too short to save,
> nor his ear too dull to hear.
> Rather, your iniquities have been barriers
> between you and your God,
> and your sins have hidden his face from you
> so that he does not hear.
> For your hands are defiled with blood,
> and your fingers with iniquity;
> your lips have spoken lies,
> your tongue mutters wickedness.
> No one brings suit justly,
> no one goes to law honestly;
> they rely on empty pleas, they speak lies,
> conceiving mischief and begetting iniquity.
>
> The way of peace they do not know,
> and there is no justice in their paths.
> Their roads they have made crooked;
> no one who walks in them knows peace.
> Therefore justice is far from us,
> and righteousness does not reach us;
> we wait for light, and lo! there is darkness;
> and for brightness, but we walk in gloom.[16]

Once again, the of lack justice has a simple cause: contrary to their public proclamations, the people don't *want* justice enough to *pursue* it. God's response is certainly not silence.

> Truth is nowhere to be found,
> and whoever shuns evil becomes a prey.
> The Lord looked and was displeased
> that there was no justice.
> He saw that there was no one,
> he was appalled that there was no one to intervene;
> so his own arm achieved salvation for him,

---

16. Isa 59:1–4, 8–9 NRSV.

and his own righteousness sustained him.
He put on righteousness as his breastplate,
and the helmet of salvation on his head;
he put on the garments of vengeance
and wrapped himself in zeal as in a cloak.[17]

Confronted with the people's inaction in the face of injustice, God chooses to act—which, as we have already noted, is a consistent theme throughout Scripture. What seems particularly striking and significant is not just divine intervention, but God's astonishment at the lack of *human* intervention.

As Israel was struggling to rebuild their city and their identity, Isaiah's statement was clear: We are meant to be people who actively practice compassion, righteousness, and justice.

Returning Home

Several days after returning from Gettysburg, still baffled by how to deal with the seemingly contradictory juxtapositions of hope and despair, joy and lament, progress and stagnation, I read the final words from *John Brown's Body*, Stephen Vincent Benét's epic poem about the Civil War:

> So, when the crowd gives tongue
> And prophets, old or young,
> Bawl out their strange despair
> Or fall in worship there,
> Let them applaud the image or condemn
> But keep your distance and your soul from them.
> And, if the heart within your breast must burst
> Like a cracked crucible and pour its steel
> White-hot before the white heat of the wheel,
> Strive to recast once more
> That attar of the ore
> In the strong mold of pain

---

17. Isa 59:15–17 NRSV.

Isaiah 56–59: Who Will We Become?

Till it is whole again,
And while the prophets shudder or adore
Before the flame, hoping it will give ear,
If you at last must have a word to say,
Say neither, in their way,
"It is a deadly magic and accursed,"
Nor "It is blest," but only "It is here."[18]

I could spend my whole life trying to untangle and make sense of what took place on that field in Pennsylvania. But to what end? At some level, I suppose this is an attempt to decide whether to call it, "a deadly magic and accursed," or to say, "it is blessed."

Our minds do not like cognitive dissonance, which is why we feel such anxiety when we are faced with what seem to be mutually exclusive realities. The easiest course is to choose which reality we prefer, and then set about gathering evidence to justify our choice—which often includes demonizing any who dare align themselves with the "other" reality. In the words of King Lear, "Oh, that way madness lies . . . No more of that." Perhaps Benét is right, and the first step away from madness is simply acknowledging, "It is here."

There resides—in a Thin Place outside of Gettysburg, in the history and the ongoing story of the United States, and even within myself—both beauty and tragedy; honor and injustice; joy and despair. To acknowledge one side and explain away the other is madness . . . no more of that.

The call to hope is not meant to silence or supplant the experience of lament. Instead, both are needed if we are to continue the fight for justice. Without hope, lament is too oppressive. Without lament, hope devolves into complacency.

The fields are still here, and the battle that took place on those fields is still here. The unfinished work and great task remaining before us are still here.

But, I am also here. And so are you.

---

18. Benét, *John Brown's Body*, 336.

I may struggle to understand what the Israelites experienced as an oppressed, displaced people. And yet, it isn't too difficult to imagine the anxiety and uncertainty tied to their questions about identity and the future. My own story—in this place, here and now—calls me to ask very similar questions. Who are we? Who are we becoming?

Embracing hope in this moment does not require us to ignore or dismiss such questions. Instead, hope encourages us to take these questions a step further and ask, "What then shall we do? Who will we *choose to be*, here and now?"

In response, we can choose to remember. "When the crowd gives tongue / and prophets, old or young, / bawl out their strange despair / or fall in worship there," we can hear that as a call to continue working. We can pursue justice wherever we are able. We can commit ourselves to looking for ways we may be complicit in exclusion. We can emphasize compassion, generosity, and concern for others.

And when we lose hope or lose focus—when we become complacent or apathetic, or give in to despair, anger, or selfishness—we can "strive to recast once more / that attar of the ore / in the strong mold of pain / Till it is whole again."

This really is a "we" thing.

If I have any chance of keeping or regaining hope, and of avoiding the pull toward self-centered egotism, it will be because I continually focus on the God who is out ahead, cultivating hope, and inviting me into that hope.

And if I have any hope of maintaining such a focus and commitment for an extended period, it will be because I seek to pursue these things in community.

So then, together, we can choose to do what we can, with whatever is here, so long as we are here. Afterwards, others can take up the work, just as we have taken it up from the ones who came before us, and just as all of us have taken it up from the one who has been, who is, and who will be working until it is finished.

I guess the final question is, "Will we?"

Notes from Denise

"How was such transcendent beauty still possible in a place so marred by violence and loss?"

This sentence leapt off the page at me. This seems such an apt description of the Story. That such transcendent beauty of people in the image of God is possible in a creation that continues to evolve and exist amid the chaos and suffering that we inflict upon each other and our planet.

It is so easy to become overwhelmed by the challenges of our current time and forget that the God who dwells among us still dwells, and that the Community we are invited into is still inviting.

It is easy to forget that God is on the move, that things can be rebuilt, that cultures can be changed, and compassion and nonviolence can overcome.

It is so easy to forget that *all* are welcome.

But we do not *have* to forget. We can choose to look, notice, and remember.

INTERLUDES ON JESUS

Jesus and the Bleeding Woman: Transforming the Community Story

Heidi A. Miller

ARDATH GREW UP AS a nominal, cradle Lutheran. She had a newly discovered faith, which awakened her afresh to Christianity right in the heart of the northern Illinois Bible Belt. She lived in an impeccable brick house, bordered by well-tended flowerbeds in an affluent north side neighborhood—directly across the street from a run-down but sturdy Cape Cod house. A scorched and blackened evergreen shrub in its front yard stood as an empirical witness to the series of renters of "that house" who had been troublemakers.

The owners, a kind Catholic family, offered to rent this house to my parents, who had just returned from mission work abroad. Most neighbors were wary of "these newcomers" who moved in with five children and little furniture. The local stigma of "that house" amplified our outsider status, and we became one more problem to be avoided.

My dad took a leave of absence from the mission board to begin working at the campus in town where he was also completing his graduate studies. My mom, a green-card-carrying immigrant from Great Britain, worked from home—typing and editing manuscripts for a local author and my dad's graduate papers on an old typewriter. The emergence of personal computers was still a few years away.

As a way of caring for and loving this new, and unwelcoming neighborhood, my mom began praying in the neighborhood as she walked. Ardath, an avid gardener who spent time outside weeding her flowerbeds, noticed her new neighbor. Ardath's little boy was the same age as one of my brothers.

Ardath, a petite woman with a carefully coiffed beehive—all the rage in the seventies—warm smile, and hearty laugh was a delightful de facto welcomer and the social glue in the community. Ardath was the first to cross the street and to welcome us to the neighborhood, inviting my parents to the monthly potluck dinners she and her husband hosted.

Over iced lemonade or, even, wine or cocktails, the potluck conversations deepened around the bar of Ardath's beautifully finished basement. Spiritual questions emerged, questions that exposed deep longings rarely expressed. Out of this, a neighborhood Bible study formed. Not just any Bible study, but one in which people strived to get serious about the Scriptures. Ardath asked, "Could we go back to the beginning, to page one, and study the Bible that way?" She longed to study the Bible in a way that opened new connections between the text and her context: between God and her life. And, so, Genesis became the book of choice. Early on, Ardath came to the Bible Study and said, "I called my extended family, my cousins and my aunts, and told them, 'There is no need to go to the movies or read novels. If you want to read about violence, sex, murder, and war, you can read Genesis.'"

The stuff of life is right there in the Scriptures.

A newcomer to the Scriptures, Ardath did not have the sanitized view of the biblical narrative common among regular churchgoers. She wrestled with God and wrestled with Scripture as she scrubbed her kitchen floor and vacuumed her carpets. She asked herself, "if Jesus came back now, what would it look like to be ready?" She evangelized through reading the biblical story and sharing about the humanity she saw there. Not for shock value. Ardath found that Scripture, the story of God with a messed-up people and a messier world, was not removed from daily life.

Instead, this story was concrete and relevant, entering the mess of her everyday world.

Shifting from Avoiding the Mess to Entering the Mess in Scripture and in Life

Much of what we hear, see, and encounter about God and the Scriptures in our culture is scrubbed clean and sanitized. An open Bible, a Holy Bible, holds a central place, a sacred spot, in the front of the sanctuary, but is rarely used. A picture of Jesus, hung up in the church foyer, shows him kneeling, relaxed in a near reclining pose. He has long brown hair, freshly cleaned and conditioned. His head is aglow as he looks heavenward. Nurseries are adorned with an ark and cute animals making their entrance, two by two, along the gangplank. Pristine figures of Mary, Joseph, and Jesus adorn our homes as we sing the Christmas carol, "The cattle are lowing the poor baby wakes, but little Lord Jesus no crying he makes."

I confess that I like nativities. A nativity scene is something I remember playing with as a child. Who would have thought that the efforts of thirteenth-century Italian monk Francis of Assisi, who called the church toward the posture of the poor to counter the materialism of his time by crafting a live, smelly nativity scene with sheep, cows, and a donkey, would become sentimental hallmarks of the Advent and Christmas season? Yet, this hallmark, like a mass-produced greeting card, has become commodified, materialized, and sanitized.

Life is messy, yet, a sanitized version of God, the Scriptures, and the church often works to keep us far from imagining a God who mucks around in the mess. The thought of this God, this Jesus, this Spirit coming and dwelling in the mess of life seems unlikely among sanitized messages promising that something will magically make everything nice and neat.

Is God a God who comes near to the mess of a family facing a child's mental illness, who refuses to leave his room, screaming obscenities at them from the other side of the door? Family and friends who mean well tell them, "Just lay down the law and discipline him." Or ask, "Are you sure he has not heard this language from you?"

The mess of a couple struggling with infertility after four years of trying, as well-meaning church friends say, "You know, when God closes a door another one opens." Or, "I am wondering, if you just relax if that would help."

The mess of a single person feeling painfully, obviously alone, finding it hard to go to church where it seems most people are sitting as a family. To make matters worse, when she walks into church the usher says, "Hey, I'm gonna' sit you by a man that is single and see what happens."

The mess of an adolescent coming out as gay, only to be told by her mother, "This is just a phase." Then, taken to a counselor who tells her, "You are ruining God's plan for your life and should pray for healing."

The mess of a couple who is divorcing after his hidden serial affairs and pornography addiction come to light. The wife is told, "Divorce is a sin," and, "You might be able to save your husband if you stay with him."

Then there are the universal messes—war, poverty, sexual abuse, and drug addiction. Each of us could add a story naming what is messy in our lives and how some have tried to sanitize it—covering it up and declaring it better.

Sanitized messages about God, the Bible, faith, and the church leave us doubting that these things have anything to do with the real world we experience every day. Many vote with their feet and leave the church. Many vote with their feet and never enter one in the first place.

Can the "sent out and on the move" God we meet in Jesus and the ongoing work of the Holy Spirit really enter the mess of our life, the life of our neighborhoods, and the life of the world? Can a missional hermeneutic and posture move us from a sanitary, easy-answer God and church, to the God who moves into our neighborhood as Jesus?

The answer in this book and in this chapter is a resounding, wholehearted, generous, this-is-tough-stuff-God-how-are-you-on-the-move yes.

Yes.

However, a shift is called for. A shift away from a gospel that is reduced to simple answers. A shift away from one Bible verse on a billboard, bumper sticker, or church sign. A shift toward a gospel that moves into the stories of our lives. Toward a gospel that crosses the street and goes places that we would sometimes rather not go—places within ourselves, in our neighborhoods, and in our churches. It means we will need to get messy as we listen to stories that are shared from the basements of our lives.

The story of the bleeding woman in the gospels (Matt 9:20–22; Mark 5:25–34; Luke 8:43–48) refuses to be sanitized. Let's enter the mess together, for reading Scripture and the stuff of life is not a private endeavor. Let's listen to the beginning of the story:

> Now when Jesus returned, the crowd welcomed him, for they were all waiting for him. Just then there came a man named Jairus, a leader of the synagogue. He fell at Jesus' feet and begged him to come to his house, for he had an only daughter, about twelve years old, who was dying.[1]

Wait a minute, I said this story is about a bleeding woman. Why are we starting with Jairus and his daughter? The story of the bleeding woman is housed within another story. All three of the accounts of the woman with the issue of blood take place within a larger story. A story within a story. Think of times when you find yourself hearing a story and it reminds you of another. Sometimes one friend will be telling a story, only to be interrupted by another friend because it reminds him of his own story. In our own culture, we find ourselves awash in the noise of narratives that compete rather than link. We are bombarded with diverse, competing stories that demand our attention. Even dining out is a competitive experience, with dozens of televisions tuned to various channels and advertisements on the wall selling products like flour, soft

---

1. Luke 8:40–42a NRSV.

drinks, and medicine for cranky infants—all snippets of stories vying for our attention, allegiance, and consumption.

The story of the bleeding woman within Jairus's story is different. This story-within-a-story is not only asking us to make links between stories, it is asking us to follow a path that leads us to a focal point, a crux-of-the-matter, turn-your-life-around plot. A life-changing plot that transforms how we see, hear, and now live within the ongoing stories of our lives.

One of the fancy ways this symmetrical storytelling pattern is referred to in literature and biblical literature is a "chiastic structure." Chai is the name of the Greek letter "X." A simple way of beginning to understand it is with the phrase "X marks the spot." All that precedes and proceeds from the core story works to move us toward the treasure at its center. All of this works together to change how we engage our lives with God, with ourselves, and with one another. The biblical storytellers want us to get inside the story and have the story get inside of us, lovingly messing with the categories and stories that shape us.

Let's continue to listen so that we can move closer to the chiastic focal story of the passage.

> As Jesus went, the crowds pressed in on him. Now there was a woman who had been suffering from hemorrhages for twelve years; and though she had spent all she had on physicians, no one could cure her. She came up behind him and touched the fringe of his clothes.[2]

I invite you to sit with this woman's reality. While getting close to her reality of bleeding and what that means in her cultural context is nearly impossible, we are beckoned to try. We are beckoned to enter the mess of her life and story. She has been menstruating for a dozen years. Her unclean flow of blood is the kind that no sanitary napkin can stop. There is that word, again, sanitary. We have difficulty talking about women's reproductive cycles in our culture. It is no coincidence that when it comes to menstruation, we hold it at a distance through convenient and polite phrases. We call it

2. Luke 8:42b–44a NRSV.

INTERLUDES—*Jesus and the Bleeding Woman*

a "period." We sell products called sanitary napkins. And we tell dismissive jokes such as, "It's her time of the month again." Perhaps it is no coincidence that she is referred to only as the woman with the hemorrhage. To get closer, even closer, I invite you to use your imagination to consider how she might tell you her story. Stop for a moment before you read any further and sit with the bloody and painful reality of this woman's life.

After you have given some time to wait with what might be arising in this story, I offer one creative option, told in a first-person narrative, to help us move closer to this woman's experience and suffering.

> It is bloody hell. My bleeding will not stop. It is constant. Twelve years now I've been unclean. Outside the camp![3] Sure, we are all unclean in some way since we are far from Jerusalem. But the uncleanliness I have does not stop. There is no stopping it. So, I am separated out, isolated, and labeled. My status is low. My wounds are high. I have no more money. I have spent it all to stop the bleeding. I've spent it all so that I could be among people in society. Oh, to be a part of something again and be clean: to sit at table again, to hold children, to embrace a family, to attend Synagogue, to join in the weddings, to join in the throng on the road to Passover.
>
> The blood, it started twelve years ago. Sure, women told me how to properly care for my menstruation and what rags to use and how to properly dispose of them. As do all faithful women, we remove ourselves when the bleeding starts. Once it stops we are cleansed and purified. Then, we can be a part of the community. The thing is, my bleeding does not stop. The flow of blood and the flow of removal from the society around me are killing me. I am as good as dead.
>
> I've heard of this teacher, this rabbi, Jesus. There is something different about him. He is different than the rabbis I have encountered—who offer me empty words

---

3. Any unclean person was required to live "outside of the camp"—until they could be cleansed and restored to the Israelite community. See Lev 12; 13:45; 15:25–30.

and platitudes that leave me weak and alone. He is different than the physicians I have seen—who take my money and offer me no cure, no relief.

There is something in Jesus that draws this woman. He draws crowds because word of him has spread throughout the region. He is known for telling stories that challenge authorities and communities. He has the reputation of not falling for the traps of debate that the religious authorities lay for him. He has been seen associating with questionable people who are on the outside of the community, even letting a so-called dubious woman wash his feet with ointment and her tears in the dining room of Simon the Pharisee. He casts out demons. He heals the sick. Who Jesus is and how Jesus is draws people toward him. *Who* he associates *with*, *how* he associates *with*, *where* he associates *with*, and *why* he associates *with* people are qualitatively different than what the woman with the hemorrhage has encountered. Jesus is *with* unclean people. He comes close to those "outside the camp" who smell. "We are called to get close enough to people to smell their stink," says Melissa, a chaplain and one of my housemates in intentional community. That's what Jesus does. He comes close. Jesus is *with* . . . God-present-*with*-us.

As you sat with the Scripture, your imagination, and the story I shared above, what happened? What are you discovering about this woman, her context, and Jesus who is on the move? What is God revealing to you?

Her story, as well as our own, does not exist apart from her or our context. Her story, and our story, is rooted in the community that surrounds her, and that surround us. Our stories happen in community. Faith happens in community. This woman's story did not come from her alone nor is it hers alone. Being rooted in the community, the story is the community's story as well. All in the community are navigating purity laws. All in the community have some level of impurity as they are living away from the temple in Jerusalem. From a practical standpoint, learning how to handle bodily fluids is a crucial part of existing in their world, as it is in ours. Instructions for going outside the village to use the latrine, as we find in Leviticus, are good if you want clean water and to prevent disease.

But something about this community's story is ruptured for this woman. Good instructions go bad. Her social dilemma, if not her physical dilemma, was born of her community. She is a product of her community. And her community has worked to eliminate her presence for its own convenience. It has cut off her story. It smells. It bleeds. And no matter how the community seeks to sanitize it, it is implicated by it. It shares the story. How might this woman's bleeding point toward a community that is bleeding? What different stories emerge to offer healing to this woman and her community?

To move toward healing, we need to listen to the other stories that are emerging. For us to be transformed by and enter into a new narrative, we need to be attentive to the narratives that have been hidden. This is why this woman's story, happening in one community then told in another and later written down in yet another, becomes so revealing. It offers us clues to how God is on the move in our own community.

The very weaving of this woman's story into the story of the temple leader's dying daughter, provides further threads of discovery. And in so doing, to borrow a phrase from Daniel Taylor's book *Tell Me a Story*, as we pull the threads of this story, maybe we will "feel the tremor half a world and two millennia away."[4]

When we read and tell this story, offering it to the next generation and the next, we do not tell it in a vacuum but within a particular context, with a particular lens. In this way the narrative is able to address a particular community. Matthew, Mark, and Luke all include this story with different nuances. From a human perspective this is not surprising since we nuance stories differently in different settings, but this may seem threatening when we are talking about something as sacred as Scripture and God's ongoing story with humanity.

---

4. Daniel Taylor offers the metaphor in the direction of beginning with our story and then moving towards the tremor "half a world and two millennia away." Taylor, *Tell Me a Story*, 6.

WHAT KIND OF GOD?

We often prefer our Scriptures straightforward and clear, without nuance, without contradiction. And when differences arise, we often can move into biblical criticism, keeping a distance from the narrative, avoiding entering in. Rather than seeing biblical complexities as something to argue about—how Scripture is or isn't inspired, is or isn't literal—I'm inviting us to enter the story. I am inviting us to observe how the gospel writers wove it together so that we would pause, take notice, and get at the turn-your-life-around reality of it.

Dwelling in the Mess: Discovering the Real Story

The new story that emerges is a story not only of healing for the woman with the hemorrhage, but also the healing of the community. We discover that, at the core of this story, the woman is not the patient, the community is.

To understand how this new story emerges, let's contrast Jairus's statement and posture with that of the woman's statement and posture as each approach Jesus amidst a large crowd by the seashore.

First, Jairus approaches Jesus in the crowd:

> Then one of the leaders of the synagogue named Jairus came and, when he saw Jesus, fell at his feet and begged him repeatedly,
>
> "My little daughter is at the point of death. Come and lay your hands on her, so that she may be made well, and live."[5]

Then, the woman approaches Jesus in the crowd:

> Now there was a woman who had been suffering from hemorrhages for twelve years. She had endured much under many physicians, and had spent all that she had; and she was no better, but rather grew worse. She had heard about Jesus, and came up behind him in the crowd and touched his cloak, for she said,

---

5. Mark 5:22–23 NRSV.

INTERLUDES—*Jesus and the Bleeding Woman*

"If I but touch his clothes, I will be made well."[6]

How does Jairus approach Jesus in the crowd? How does the woman approach Jesus in the crowd? Did you notice how Jairus seems to approach Jesus directly while the woman approaches Jesus from behind? These are two different postures, two different statuses, two different ways of getting to Jesus in a crowd. Jairus has power in the community, this woman does not.

I feel the pull of the thread over two millennia away. A missional lens is asking us an important question not to be missed. Who holds the power in our communities? Whose voice gets heard? Whose voice gets silenced? Let's get even closer, and perhaps more uncomfortable: Who holds the power in our church? Whose voice gets heard? Whose voice gets silenced? What is talked about in the church? What is not talked about in the church? Who has ready access to power, to money, to position? Who gets separated from the church? Who is in? Who is out?

Let's visit a new story that pulls on the two-thousand-year-old thread. Adam, Ashley, Matthew, and Catherine, a team that is part of the Missional Wisdom Foundation, live in Wichita, Kansas. They live in intentional community *with* the wider community in a neighborhood labeled, by those outside and inside the neighborhood, as the "bad section" of town. This story gets communicated and repeated in myriad ways:

"Why would you want to live there?"

"You would not want to live in that part of town."

"That part of town has drugs and prostitutes and more."

"Investing in housing in that area is not a good idea."

Even the social service agencies and nonprofit agencies fall into this kind of storytelling:

"There is nothing good in that neighborhood."

"Investing in that eleven-year-old child from that neighborhood will never work out."

"That neighborhood does not want to change."

---

6. Mark 5:25–28 NRSV.

Do you hear the story? The categories of bad: drugs, prostitutes, lazy, hopeless, etc., label this community.

What if there is a different way to approach this community? What if this story is not *the* Story of this community? What if the Holy Spirit of God is already on the move in this neighborhood?

Let's return to the gospel story. What if there is a different way of noticing the bleeding woman? What if her bleeding is not *the* Story? This is not to put aside her bleeding, pain, and wounds, but rather be *with* her: see her, notice her, look at what is happening in and through all of her. What if the Spirit of God, present in Jesus, is on the move *in* and *with* her and *in* and *with* her neighborhood? What might we notice? What if there is a different story that is emerging in this story-within-a-story?

Jairus, falling at Jesus's feet, begs him, "Come and lay your hands on her, so that she may be made well, and live."

The woman says, "If I but touch his cloak, I will be made well."

Both are drawn to Jesus. Both sense Jesus has something to offer. Yet, the storyteller wants us to get ahold of something crucial. This woman is showing strength.

Strengths? What? This woman, wounded and bleeding, has strengths? Really? Her body is weak. Her skin is pale and gaunt. She is unclean. What do you mean, strengths?

What might this woman's strengths show us about how God's Spirit, present in Jesus, is on the move in and through her? The writers of this story, by embedding it in the story of Jairus's daughter, want us to hear her story in relationship with Jairus's story. Pause, for a moment, come closer and notice the strength of this disabled woman:

- She pays attention to the stories of Jesus, so much so that she seeks him out.
- She is willing to take a risk.
- She is tenacious.
- She is courageous.
- She refuses to be separated out.

- She uses her all her might to get to Jesus.
- She initiates the touch.
- She does not want the spotlight.
- She does not even need to touch his skin to receive something from him.
- She is an overcomer.
- She shows great faith.

What might the power of noticing the gifts already present *with* and *in* this woman offer the community? What might she have to teach the community? Her tenacity and her faith offer the community a way of learning how to overcome and persist, even with God, when all seems lost.

Now back to Kansas. What might the power of noticing the gifts already present *with* and *in* people offer the Wichita community? What might the power of noticing the presence and movement of God's Spirit offer the Wichita community? Our friends Adam, Ashley, Matthew, and Catherine would love to share it with you. They developed a nonprofit organization called SoCe Life to be *with* this community and draw this community to be *with* one another. They believe, "God has gifted everyone, and as individuals share their gifts for the benefit of others, they experience wholeness and the community becomes stronger."[7]

They put on their walking shoes and go door to door, getting to know their neighbors. The goal is to hear about each person's gifts, abilities, and strengths. Catherine says that people are reticent and wary of them at first. The question at the door, "Can we interview you about your gifts and strengths," is frequently met with a perplexed, "I don't think I have any." Kindly, Catherine says, "We believe everyone is gifted." Curiously and cautiously, one neighbor—we'll call her Grace—allowed Catherine to come into her home to ask her questions. An hour later Catherine and Grace have a list of eighteen strengths they discover through Grace's stories.

---

7. See http://www.socelife.org/aboutus/.

Grace shares that she would love to learn how to cook. Catherine asks permission to share her name with another neighbor in the community, who used to be a chef in Cuba—we'll call her Isabel—who has been looking for more opportunities to share her love of cooking. Soon people in the community are enjoying Isabel and Grace's food and begin spreading the word about a new catering service.

This kind of neighboring allows a different story to emerge, one that is based on strengths, giftedness, and what someone offers the community in the midst of the mess of life. Furthermore, it allows each person, and the community as a whole, to become active in their own story. The gifts of these two talented women, discovered and empowered over time, offer grace with and in the neighborhood. Rather than isolation and loneliness, this kind of neighboring draws people together in community. The narrative of the community is given space to shift, and, out of that new narrative, new life emerges. The potential of what this community offers the wider city of Wichita, not as "patient" of the city but as healing gift, is profound.

Let's wander into the SoCe Life Center at the heart of this community. We will notice how the center's work in discovering stories, identifying strengths, and bringing those strengths and stories together, point to a treasure at the core of the neighborhood.

Outside the SoCe Center, garden boxes are being constructed for the front yards of neighbors in the community. Inside, along with tables, chairs, and easy chairs there is a map of the streets in the community covering a whole wall. It is not the kind of a map that plots land, but rather one that plots strengths and gifts. The homes are marked with yellow sticky tabs. On the sticky tabs are lists of gifts and strengths of people in that particular home. This tells a different story; a different plot being woven together over time. Another narrative is being cultivated in this community. One in which Jesus is on the move in the neighborhood in the midst of the mess and beauty of real people and real life. X marks the spot.

As we return to the story of the bleeding woman, we begin to get a sense of the profound desperation and the profound strength

INTERLUDES—*Jesus and the Bleeding Woman*

she has to reach out in the midst of a community that labeled her worthless. This woman, on the fringe of society, reaches out and touches the fringe of Jesus's garment.

> She came up behind him and touched the fringe of his clothes, and immediately her hemorrhage stopped. Then Jesus asked, "Who touched me?" When all denied it, Peter said, "Master, the crowds surround you and press in on you." But Jesus said, "Someone touched me; for I noticed that power had gone out from me."[8]

In the moment of reaching out and touching the fringe of Jesus's garment, running it quickly against her fingertips, the woman is healed. This woman's bleeding stops.

Jesus stops. Jesus notices. Jesus's body notices that he has been touched. Not the jostling touches of the crowd, but the touch of someone whom his body recognizes. Jesus calls out, "Who touched me?" He acknowledges her touch, naming the very thing—touch—that is not allowed. Touch, as Miroslav Volf says, draws us "into existence" as humans.[9] We are touched into being on this earth as an infant. Without touch, we cannot live and grow in this world. As this woman shares her existence and touches Jesus her in the midst of her uncontrollable bleeding, his body acknowledges her and meets her where she is, in the mess and reality of her bleeding and giftedness. Jesus lets go of power in his body and gives her his power in her body.

What happens for you as you sit with the phrase, "touch draws us into existence as humans?"

While this points to the sacredness, the hallowed reality of touch, it is important to recognize that not all touch is good touch, healthy touch, or welcomed touch. Many have been wronged by touch. Wounds from abusive touch, physical and sexual, run deep—very deep. Abusive touch harms to the core, fragmenting us on the deepest of levels. It does the opposite of bringing the person into existence. Abusive touch denies the existence of the person.

---

8. Luke 8:44–46 NRSV.
9. Volf, "Redemption of Touch."

WHAT KIND OF GOD?

As we continue to pause, to stop, and to notice, echoing Jesus's response to the woman's touch, acknowledging the hallowed reality of touch, what happens for you when you hear the phrase: Jesus is bodily present with this woman and meets her where she is? What might it mean for you to allow Jesus to join you and meet you where you are? How might Jesus join you in the midst of hallowed, wounded places? How might you be invited to be bodily present with others where they are? Take some time with these questions. Notice the invitation that arises.

Instead of allowing this woman and her touch to fade into the distance, Jesus is going to have this woman tell her story in community. Jesus wants her to be seen and heard. Her journey into fuller existence is not over.

> When the woman saw that she could not remain hidden, she came trembling; and falling down before him, she declared in the presence of all the people why she had touched him, and how she had been immediately healed. He said to her, "Daughter, your faith has made you well; go in peace."[10]

This time, when the woman approaches Jesus, she does so from the front, falling at Jesus's feet. Her posture is shifting, much closer to that of Jairus's in the early part of the narrative. A shift is happening in her narrative in the presence of Jesus and in the presence of the community. Jesus wants her to be seen and heard. She is somebody! She has a story that needs to be shared. She has a story that needs to be heard.

Jesus does not recoil from the woman. Jesus gets closer to her. Jesus gets so close, he calls her family, "Daughter." Daughter! She is family in God's community. She belongs. The one who was on the outside is actually on the inside. She has a place.

The journey of Jesus's empowerment is not over as we come close to the heart of it, to the X that marks the spot, "Your faith has made you well; go in peace." It is at this point in the text that we celebrate. What are we celebrating? Most of us will answer, "We

---

10. Luke 8:47–48 NRSV.

are celebrating this woman's faith." Then draw the conclusion that if we have faith then healing will happen. Therefore, have faith.

No. This is not the story. This approach, this one-liner conclusion at the "X marks the spot," misses the point. This simplistic answer makes the woman the patient. She is not the patient in this story, the community is the patient. What? Are you sure? She is the one who was sick. She is the one who was bleeding. Yes, she was bleeding and sick, but the community is bleeding and far sicker. They have been telling and living into a sick story.

This community sees her disease as a weakness and attributes it to her lack of faith. Jesus flips the entire power structure upside down when he makes this declaration. This woman who touched Jesus and receives the power of his body is the one who has power. She has the faith the community needs. A faith, not some distant thing to be grasped, but one that is enacted and embodied. The community needs all that this woman has to offer. She is a powerful gift that the community needs.

This healing and all healing in the Scripture is not for an individual alone, but rather for the entire community. This missional lens of healing and allowing Scripture to read us, brings us back to Kansas. The healing of each person's story and each neighborhood's story happens within that community and for the greater community. Something in the cities of our lives need healing, and Jesus is showing us how to show up, be present, and notice those already in place to embody that healing.

I invite you into the image of a stone thrown into a pond. Ripples form around the stone, expanding ever wider. A missional reading of the Scripture is much like this stone thrown into a pond. At the center is the triune God, who is at work in the neighborhood of the Scripture, making waves that ripple into our time and "read us" in our context. Our incarnational God continues to make ripples in the neighborhood of our lives, calling us to show up, be present, and notice. Our incarnational God continues to make ripples in, with, and through our neighbors and in our neighborhoods. Finally, we are not to stay outside of the pond. We are called to be in the pond, joining with the ripples of God.

WHAT KIND OF GOD?

Notes from Denise

And now we see that building our Temple to contain the Community is inconsistent with the God who is in the mess with each of us. We are challenged to see that mess is all around us in the Story.

Why do we have such a hard time recognizing that the messes in the Bible are often not fundamentally very different from the messes of our own very messy, very human lives? And why do we struggle to acknowledge that this is okay?

If Jesus can enter the unclean messes, who are we to avoid the muck, think we should somehow be immune to the muck, or join in the comparison of whether my muck is better than your muck?

Can we learn to get close enough to smell the stink—and recognize how we ourselves have contributed?

Can we resist the urge to judge the muck, both our own and that of others?

John 4: "I Am" Sent Her

Larry Duggins

I (Larry) consider my years at the SMU Perkins School of Theology as one of the greatest gifts God has given me. I came to Perkins as a real live grown-up—I turned fifty during my first semester there—and I had done some pretty high flying as an entrepreneur and business leader. God called me away from practically everything I knew and sat me down in a lecture class, shifting me from a President and COO to a graduate student. My whole frame of reference began to shift, and I entered the second half of life.

I was surrounded by wonderful classmates, bright people both young and old who are still some of my dearest friends. My church and my family worked to process my shifting perspectives, helping me to embrace something new. I read voraciously, trying to actually *absorb* every assignment rather than lapsing into the graduate-school skim.

And I was blessed with an amazing group of teachers—during my time at Perkins I learned from a Filipino Jesuit Buddhist, a Latino who ran a church of undocumented Christians, and a maverick Evangelism professor who became my partner in ministry for eight years before she became the Dean of Duke Divinity School. And I learned from Jaime (pronounced like "jay-me") Clark-Soles, who taught me to love the Book of John.

WHAT KIND OF GOD?

Jaime is quite a character—she is a world-renowned authority on John, a simultaneously challenging and freedom-giving teacher, and a strong woman with a prophetic voice. And she can kick your butt in racquetball. I took a seminar on John from her and watched with joy as she taught us to peel back layer after layer, revealing more and more about Jesus and his life. I learned that every detail in John is important, and that revisiting John is like watching a movie you love—every time you see it, you notice something new. So, when Jaime recently published a new book on the Book of John,[1] I preordered it.

In her discussion of the story of the woman at the well, Jaime points out the different ways that Jesus uses the term "I Am" in the Gospel of John. In many cases, Jesus uses the term to establish a metaphor that describes an aspect of Jesus's role in the world. When he says "I am the light of the world" in John 8:12, he is not implying that he has physically become a celestial light bulb, but rather that he is a source of spiritual illumination. When he says "I am the gate of the sheep" in John 10:7, he is referring to himself as the source of access to salvation, not as a physical component of livestock fencing. This metaphorical use of "I am" parallels another way Jesus uses the phrase.

In his conversation with the woman at the well, Jesus's responses to the woman's questions reach consistently deeper than the questions themselves seem to require. When she questions why he would ask her for water—a very counter-cultural act on his part—he responds by asking her whether she knows with whom she is speaking and whether she is aware that the great blessing of living water is available to her. When she takes him literally and asks where his bucket is, he responds that the water he gives is a spring of eternal life. When she asks for this water so that she will never have to, ever, draw water again, he reveals that he knows more about her than she is aware. When she calls him a prophet and challenges him to solve a historical theological dilemma, he responds that distinctions like the one she raises have become irrelevant because God the Father is seeking those who worship in

1. Clark-Soles, *Reading John*.

spirit and truth. When she replies that the Messiah is coming, he says: "I am."

This whirlwind of ever-strengthening questions and answers culminates in Jesus explicitly naming himself in precisely the same way that God names Godself in a conversation with Moses in Exodus 3. In that passage, Moses has encountered the Burning Bush and initiated his own whirlwind of questions centering around whether he was the right person for God to send to liberate the Jews from Egyptian captivity. In verse 13, Moses asks the Bush a conditional question—"IF I choose to go, who shall I say sent me?" The Bush answers "I am who I am—tell them 'I am' has sent you." Jesus echoes these words to the woman at the well, stating in no uncertain terms that the Messiah—the Son of God—was in her presence. This is different than the instructional word-pictures that Jesus combined with powerful signs to teach the crowds to believe. This is Jesus saying directly to a person—a Samaritan woman, mind you—that "I am" God.

In seminary-speak, we might say that the Book of John has a "high Christology"—that John clearly sees Jesus as divine. From the very beginning of the book, John describes Jesus as God, so this passage might be interpreted as one of several such statements by or about Jesus. But Jaime suggests that we shift our perspective to the woman who, according to verse 28, put down her water jar and went into the city.

Now, if we are feeling judgmental, we can read between the lines to draw all kinds of conclusions about the woman. Does the fact that she has had five husbands and is now living with a sixth man mean that she is sexually promiscuous or simply unlucky? Does the fact that she came alone to the well mean that she is a social outcast or simply running behind that day? Does her willingness to engage a foreign man in discussion mean that she is brazen and seductive or simply lonely? Do her intelligent questions mean that she does not know her place or that she is truly curious? If we choose to be fair, we do not have enough evidence from the passage itself to draw conclusions about the morality of the woman. We can, however, draw some insight from her actions.

WHAT KIND OF GOD?

Drawing water for the day was serious business for the women of that time. Water for cooking, cleaning, and drinking had to be drawn daily for the operation of the household. It was heavy, tedious work, but it was a critical function that could not be neglected without a negative impact on herself and her household. Yet her encounter with Jesus was so profound that she put aside her critical work for the day. Her engagement with God interrupted her daily routine, and she set aside her usual tasks to react and respond to Jesus.

When she encountered Jesus, she did not keep the experience to herself. It would be quite easy to imagine the woman simply swinging her water jar to her shoulder and heading home a little more slowly, thinking about the words of Jesus. Those words may have even eventually transformed her perspective, bringing about a new emphasis on moral living and religious observance. That is not what happened. The woman hurries back to Sychar to tell the townspeople what happened and invite them to encounter Jesus for themselves and decide if he might be the Messiah. Verses 41 and 42 tell us that many people from the city came to believe, not because of the woman's words but because she invited them to hear Jesus for themselves.

Last night, I was sitting in front of the television watching one of the college football playoff games. The score was unexpectedly close, and I was all settled in with a fire in the fireplace, a fuzzy blanket over my legs, and an appropriate adult beverage. So, when my three-year-old granddaughter asked me to read her a book, I politely declined.

She wandered off and I began to wonder about the cost of my unwillingness to set my routine aside. I muted the TV (I will admit that I did press the record button), and I called her back over. She crawled into my lap and snuggled up, and we had a wonderful time reading about Mickey Mouse, numbers, and the alphabet. I would have completely missed that experience if I had just stayed with my routine, and I would not have had a story to share with you. The woman was smart enough to realize that something important was happening to her, and she chose not to ignore it.

INTERLUDES—*John 4: "I Am" Sent Her*

As Americans, we are especially prone to prioritize work over everything else. I have both watched and experienced families suffering because the business-demands of Mom's or Dad's work took priority over a family event. I have left hospital rooms too quickly because, with five more room-calls to make, I did not have time to listen to another story. But, surprise, surprise—the Holy Spirit is not bound by our work schedule. The woman teaches us that when God speaks, the result may involve a change of plans and perspective.

During my first week at Perkins, I was asked to read a short story about a pastor in a suburban Virginia neighborhood. He was gardening in his backyard when he heard the audible voice of God tell him to change the outreach of his church to include their poor neighbors. The pastor was very confused by this experience, and wondered how to explain it to his wife and congregation in a way that avoided them pronouncing him insane.

Our professor asked us to discuss this dilemma with our classmates at our tables. I was sitting with two African American women (I am a white man) and we sat for a minute or two in that awkward I-don't-really-know-you-too-well-yet-so-I-really-don't-want-to-speak-first silence. To break the ice, I said, "Well, I kind of empathize with the pastor. It must be quite a shock to hear the voice of God." They looked at me like I was from another planet and said, "God talks to us all the time!" We all laughed and had a great chat, and I found two new friends with a different perspective than mine.

The woman at the well did not keep her story to herself. She hurried back into town and she told her own story and the impact it had on her. Note that the woman did not rush back to town condemning the sinful behavior of all her neighbors—instead, she testified about her discussion and experience with Jesus, and she invited her neighbors to come experience him for themselves. She shared *her* own experience in a way that offered her neighbors the opportunity to encounter Jesus on *their* own. The Scripture tells us that many believed because they were invited by the woman to come meet Jesus.

This little story sheds a bright light on the importance of being aware of the power of the reader's perspective. It is entirely possible to encounter this Scripture in a way that condemns the sinfulness of the woman, emphasizes the artfulness of Jesus's words in overcoming her sinful resistance, and highlights the miraculous transformation of the sinful woman into a successful proselytizer. A missional reading asks us to look at the situation through Jesus's eyes and to assume his stance as one who loves people. Reading this passage from the missional perspective shifts us away from condemnation to compassion.

It is possible to see the woman as one of us, a neighbor who has had a hard time, and who is struggling to find security and companionship. We can see Jesus breaking through social and economic barriers to encounter her in a way that she finds shocking but not threatening. Jesus patiently walks with her through her defensive and potentially offensive questions, answering in a gentle, methodical way that leads the woman closer to the gospel. He lays open his knowledge of her life in a way that allows repentance and forgiveness, if it is necessary, while affirming her response. Finally, when she is ready, Jesus reveals himself to her directly and she believes.

The story also outlines a highly missional response from the woman. She sets aside the traditional roles that typically demanded her time and energy to be responsive to the call given her. She took her message to her neighbors: to the people in her community. She spoke about Jesus's impact on and revelation into her life, and she invited them to encounter Jesus just as she did—through discussion and engagement, not shaming and coercion. Her truth-filled simple testimony about her personal experience with Jesus led to the belief of many.

A missional reading that flows from the perspective of Jesus's love instead of God's judgment and condemnation transforms this story from Jesus manipulating this woman into a confession of guilt, to a theology-twisting, rule-rewriting missional encounter viewed through the lens of "I Am."

INTERLUDES—*John 4: "I Am" Sent Her*

Here's the missional synopsis—God initiates contact with a human, reaching through cultural barriers to speak to a woman who is a possible outcast. God is patient with her, answering her objections, exposing her weakness without exploiting it, offering her the chance to enter relationship. God sticks with it until the woman, using her own mind and her own will, chooses to embrace God and to share the Good News. And let's not overlook what God did not do. God did not choose to speak to the village elder. God did not even choose to speak to a man. God did not issue an edict to the woman or condemn her questioning or past behavior. God did not even wait for her to come looking for him. God approached her.

As a missional reader, I often try to identify the steps Jesus takes as an example for my own behavior. In looking at the actions of Jesus in his encounter with the woman, I might be able to draw out a few observations to consider:

- It is okay to initiate the conversation.
- Truth-filled compassion goes much further than accusation.
- All people are worth talking to.

At least, that is what stands out for me.

One of the many benefits of reading the Bible in community is that we have access to more insights and perspectives. So, I wonder, what do you notice as you consider Jesus's actions in this encounter?

Notes from Denise

Stories.

It's all about the stories within the Story. How have we missed that? The story of the woman at the well has so very many levels—making it a great example of the importance and value of stories. Larry's story about coming to ministry and how that informed his experience of seminary and classmates; the real-to-life example of how our everyday walking-around life is part of the Story, just as the everyday trip to the well was for the Samaritan woman.

And look at the transformation that occurred. How often do we walk through our day and miss the conversations, or relationships, or experiences that have the power to transform us?

What if we embraced the idea that our story is part of the Story?

What if we embraced the idea that the same is true for all of us together?

Philippians 2: To Want and to Do

Larry Duggins

STUDYING SCRIPTURE DURING THEOLOGICAL education is a funny thing. Sometimes I would encounter a Scripture I thought that I knew, only to find that its historical context completely changed its meaning for me. Other times, I would see new layers to a Scripture that I had not seen at all. The best times, though, were when I found a Scripture passage that I had never seriously encountered before, and it changed and shaped me. The first half of Philippians 2 is such a passage.

The chapter begins mid-rant. Paul is writing to the people of the church at Philippi from prison, and he is preaching about how his misfortune has been an opportunity for him to advance the gospel. He shifts from his own story to urge the Philippians to stand firm in their faith and to not waiver in the face of opposition. He teaches that the Philippians have the privilege of believing and suffering for Jesus's sake. And as chapter 2 starts, Paul takes a breath. You can imagine him leaning back into his chair, calming down for a second or two, and starting again in a calm, firm voice.

Make me happy, he teaches, by being unified. Think the same way, love the same way, being together and agreeing with each other. The words convict me every time I read them. In this world, in this country, in this church, it seems like all we can do is disagree and fight. Do we welcome people of different races and colors or violently exclude them? Do we help people to legally find work and new homes or do we build walls and throw "illegals" out as fast as we can catch them? What in the world do we do with gays and lesbians and trans-people and bi-people and all those other folks who are so different from me?

And Paul does not stop there. He says don't be selfish, but rather think of others as better than you. Them? Those people? Don't watch out for yourself, but rather think about what is good for the other. Them? Those people?

And then he tops it off with a challenge to follow the example of Jesus. Jesus, who is really and truly God, but who chose not to exploit his personal power. Jesus, who chose to become a lowly, poor human. Jesus, who obeyed God so closely, even when his obedience led to torture, humiliation, and death. Jesus, who is Lord.

Yet Paul calls for the Philippians to stand strong, to shine like stars among those who are crooked and corrupt. Paul says that even if he is poured out like a drink offering on the altar, he will be glad. God enables us to both want to stand strong and to actually live out the life he calls us to.

Do you see what I did in that last paragraph? I shifted from thinking about Philippians to thinking about us, because that's what missional readers of Scripture do. What is Paul saying to us, and how is the Holy Spirit prompting us to use this Scripture in life today?

Paul's instruction begins with a call to unity—think the same way, love the same way, be together and agree. At first blush, that can seem scary. After all, we have all encountered religious groups who throw out anyone who does not agree with them or who varies from the set of rules or beliefs they establish. Through my missional lens, I do not think that is what he is referring to. In his first letter to the Corinthians, Paul calls out the people of Corinth for breaking into factions related to the specific teachings of different teachers.[1] He reminds them that Jesus is Lord and the center of Christian belief, and I believe Paul is making a similar statement to the Philippians. I am taking a hint from Philippians 1:9–10 in

---

1. See 1 Cor 1:10–17.

INTERLUDES—*Philippians 2: To Want and to Do*

which Paul prays that they might have knowledge and insight so that they will be able to decide what truly matters. I think that Paul was calling the Philippians to focus on the gifts and example of Jesus rather than getting tangled up in the minutiae of belief.

That does not mean that missional people should not have strongly held beliefs. Rather, it suggests that as Christian people we should allow others to hold their beliefs strongly too, with a focus on the centrality of Jesus. In his sermon "Catholic Spirit," John Wesley proposes that Christians should embrace one another if "the heart is right." That spirit of allowing difference of interpretation in specific belief around the core of Jesus' teaching allows us to be welcoming, open, and inclusive. Paul calls the Philippians—and us—to walk together toward Jesus.

Reverend Eric Conklin lives in Portland, Oregon, with his wife, Mira, and their son, Auggie. While they both work in community development, Mira is leading a Missional Wisdom Launch & Lead group in the Portland area, and Eric is helping the MWF Portland hub come to life. Here are Eric's thoughts about walking together toward Jesus in Portland:

> We are excited to be a part of the development of something ancient and new in the city of Portland. As my friends in the Evangelical Lutheran Church in America (ELCA) have reminded me, this coming year will mark the 500th anniversary of the Lutheran reformation. We are seeking to learn what re-formation God is up to in the Portland region.
>
> Speaking to the ecumenism that is breathing new life into leadership development in Portland, the community that we and three of our friends are forming in the northeast Portland neighborhood of Cully will be anchored to two neighborhood ELCA Churches (Salt and Light Lutheran Church, out of the Leaven Community, and Luther Memorial Church) with Eric's secondary deacon appointment supported by the Rose City Park United Methodist Church. This community is forming in a duplex directly across from Hacienda Community Development Corporation-sponsored low-income housing for immigrants primarily from Latin American and

African countries. With a Rule of Life as a guide, the intention is to share space and life rhythms, including meals, spiritual practices and gatherings, mutual care for our rented property, and to intentionally build relationships with neighbors, especially those who are on the margins. We will practice cultivating inward and outward relationships, will practice hospitality, justice, and interdependence with our neighbors and will explore how our individual and community vocations call us daily to live with intention where we are. As we grow in our practice as community, we dream of enough space to invite others in, to learn and be formed by being community.[2]

Furthermore, the Missional Wisdom Foundation is in conversation with three healthy United Methodist Churches who have parsonages that are not being used by their pastors and whose congregations have a vision and capacity for re-seeing Jesus in their neighborhood. One of those churches, Fremont UMC, already has the three main ingredients for making this a reality: pastoral commitment, church members who want to live in community, and available property! Our work in the Missional Wisdom Foundation will be to ground this growing group in their relationship with God and with one another and provide financing, training, and education to sustain the local ministries for the long haul.

The partnerships that we have already experienced in northeast Portland have been extremely fruitful. In this city, people of varying household incomes are rarely encouraged to engage with one another, and racial inequality takes the forms of neighborhood gentrification and isolation toward non-urban communities outside of Portland. It is increasingly difficult for many low-to-middle income families to imagine how they will stay within the city limits. In addition, people of all life experiences and backgrounds experience isolation and separation, and we seek real, person-to-person community at the neighborhood level to create a new narrative. Rooted in love, if we can learn to truly see one another, to hear and know one another's stories, to lift the gifts that are already

---

2. Missional Wisdom Foundation to "Wisdom for the Way" mailing list, July 27, 2016. To subscribe to Wisdom for the Way, visit: bit.ly/WisdomWay.

INTERLUDES—*Philippians 2: To Want and to Do*

present and listen together for the ways the Spirit is already at work where we are, we can be transformed and transform. Through the building of relationships with neighbors, we can act together to powerfully create the kind of community we all dream of, neighborhood by neighborhood.

Paul goes further than simply counseling us to avoid factionalism. He teaches that the Philippians should turn away from selfishness and self-centeredness, and they should believe others are better than they are and that they should put the interests of others before their own. This must have been hard for the Philippians to hear, but it seems even harder for us, especially those of us who are Americans. Isn't America the greatest country on earth? Doesn't capitalism teach us that if everyone will look out for their own self-interest, everyone will do better?

That is not what Paul teaches. Paul calls for humility, saying that we should look to the worth of others without regard to our own claims to status. Paul asks that we set our self-interest aside, looking instead to the self-interest of others. And this, dear missional friends, is a hard teaching. This teaching says that we can't build a wall to keep those who are not worthy away. This teaching says that we need to look to the needs of those who are asking for help, even if it means that our jobs are affected. This teaching says that we cannot hoard our own resources when others are in need. This is a hard teaching.

Ryan Klinck, the house steward of the Missional Wisdom Foundation's Bonhoeffer House in Dallas, tells a story of the fruit of releasing his authority to his homeless neighbors:

> Over the summer, I had done a lot of work to empower the members of the house, along with empowering some of the people involved in the community of the house. This has included putting some of the homeless guys into leadership of the ministry of the house, which they have taken upon themselves. An example of this is seeing them invest in the house by coming up with their own projects to make the house look better.
>
> All of this came together in a beautiful way last night. We had some new homeless men come to the

house who had never been to the house before. One of our guys, Mike, took them under his wing, welcomed them, showed them where the clothing closet was, sat with them at the table, and gave them advice on how to not get their stuff stolen. When I met Mike about two years ago, he mostly kept to himself, did not trust too many people, and especially did not want to have much of anything to do with church. It is incredible to see him now years later, leading within the community and creating a safe space for others to come into our house by loving on them, but also protecting the house.[3]

Our houses make such a significant difference in people's lives, and I am astounded by how just developing deep friendships and real relationships brings about such wonderful fruit!

Paul then lifts the example of Jesus, and the hard teaching becomes even stronger. The biblical text itself suggests that Paul is invoking a hymn, a song used in worship that the readers might have been familiar with. The hymn tells a story of self-emptying and sacrifice that leads to the salvation of the world.

The hymn begins by proclaiming Jesus as being equal to God, and yet choosing not to exploit that power. That alone is mind-boggling. It is hard to imagine a person having a better claim to be high and mighty, yet Jesus chose to set that power aside. I know that when I try to imagine myself with that kind of power, it typically involves me swooping in to save the day or to crush some oppressive force. Not so with Jesus—the power is his, yet he chose not to exploit it.

In fact, he chose to become one of us. He chose to become a poor Palestinian Jew who became a refugee as a baby when his family ran to Egypt to escape the murderous King Herod. He grew up in an occupied land, brown-skinned and sweaty from working with his hands, and he chose to walk with the lowlifes and the sinners whom he encountered. Jesus chose this. God chose this.

And in his humility, he was obedient to God even when it led to torture and an agonizingly slow death. He set aside the power

---

3. Ryan Klinck, email correspondence, August, 18, 2016.

that could have saved him to save those who were lower than him—to prove that love always wins. The hymn concludes with the Good News that the humble one is the Christ, the Lord, to the glory of God the Father.

All of which makes it a bit more difficult to place our personal safety and national security above all else.

The song Paul uses in this Scripture is sometimes called the Hymn of Kenosis after its central usage of a Greek word that is often translated as "pouring out" or "letting go." I have written elsewhere about the implications of pouring out,[4] so I would like to dwell for a second with "letting go." It seems that most of us move through life these days with an agenda; a list of tasks and objectives to be satisfied and obtained. Jesus emptied himself, letting go of his personal agenda and concerns to embrace those of the Father. This is humility that reaches soul-deep, not just humble words or postures, but a release of ego to its core, an embrace of the causes of God as the only focus of activity.

Paul concludes this portion of his letter with a summary of why all these things are important. Each of us, he says, should carry out our own salvation. He lets us know that God helps us want to live out his good purposes, and to do so. To want to, and to actually do it. What a mandate for the missional reader—we are blessed to want to do God's good work in the world, and we are given the means to do it. No couch potatoes here—we are called to be people of action, giving of ourselves deeply to do God's work in the world.

Notes from Denise

"Make me happy, he teaches, by being unified. Think the same way, love the same way, being together and agreeing with each other."

Drop the mic. What else do we need to be reminded of? Love your neighbor, love your enemy, love, love, love, love—in a self-giving and humble way—just the way Jesus showed us all how to do.

4. Please see Duggins, *Simple Harmony*.

5

Philippians 4:4–9: Think about Such Things

What You See Is What You Get

I DON'T KNOW IF you have ever spent much time thinking about it, but "what you see is what you get" is an interesting little phrase. Like many things, this statement can have different connotations depending on the speaker's delivery and the hearer's perspective.

For some, "what you see is what you get" is more commonly encountered as WYSIWYG—pronounced "wizzy-wig." This nonsense word is actually an acronym used by bloggers, website designers, and others who create content on the web. It refers to a simplified page creation tool that looks a lot like standard word processing and publishing software. If, while writing a blog post on your Macbook, you select a section of text and hit "command-b," those words will turn bold on your screen and will look the same when published. If you click an icon at the top of the page to italicize a word or change font size or type a colon and a close-parenthesis together to insert a smiley-face emoticon, that is exactly how it will look when someone views it from their laptop in Ontario, a desktop in Kenya, or a smartphone in Hong Kong.

WHAT KIND OF GOD?

If that sounds ridiculously obvious, you can thank Wizzywig. Before the creation of that feature, you would need to manually insert the emphasis HTML tag just to get a bold font. Want to insert that little smiley face emoji? You would need to insert the image tag: <img src="smiley.gif" alt="Smiley face" width="42" height="42">.

How about including a <p> for each new paragraph?

Our friend Wizzywig, though not nearly as precise or powerful as a more technical approach, makes it possible for the average Internet user to become an online contributor. It means you don't have to know HTML, CSS, Java or other coding languages to tell your computer how to display your content.

WYSIWYG is generally received with gratitude and a sigh of relief. It means simplicity and a more level playing field. But that isn't the only definition, is it? For many of us, "what you see is what you get," denotes a claim of authenticity, transparency, and a lack of posturing or deceptive theatrics. It is a way of saying that someone doesn't put on a show to impress, doesn't pretend to be something they're not, and is content to be accepted or rejected for who they are—which, they believe, is plainly evident to all they meet.

To others it has a slightly different connotation: "Don't ask for upgrades, discounts, refunds, or warranties. This is the offer, take it or leave it." Those operating from a paradigm of suspicion will hear the phrase as an indicator that someone is trying to get rid of a broken item.

This short list of common uses and interpretations is far from exhaustive, and examples (in one form or another) can be found in many contexts. In fact, I'd like to suggest that the Apostle Paul, in the conclusion to his letter to the Philippian church, provides us with an extremely powerful and valuable way to understand good old Wizzywig.

Philippians 4:4–9: Think about Such Things

Shaped by Our Story and Stories

I don't know what stories have shaped you and brought you to this present moment. Even though I am confident that if we were to sit down and share a beverage we could find some points of connection and overlap, I also suspect we would find a great deal of diversity as well.

Perhaps you did not grow up participating in worship services or in a family that read the Bible very often—or ever. On the other hand, maybe you've spent every Sunday since birth occupying the same pew and the pages of your Bible are showing more wear than my son's lucky pants (I shake my head in wonder every time those pants come out of the dryer intact).

Though not a perfect match, my story more closely resembles that latter example. And even among those who would say the same there is still a lot of variety. My wife and I—both raised in Christian homes from the same faith tradition—have a significant amount of divergence in how those similar stories played out.

Growing up, if my friends and I were to take bets on what Scripture passages would serve as sermon material on a given week (not that we would ever have done such a thing . . . publicly), the smart money would have been on one or more of Paul's writings.

More than the gospels and definitely more than anything in the two-thirds of the Bible that precede Matthew, it was Paul who consistently got the most airtime. Though our church was nowhere near as combative and legalistic as many from our tradition, we still turned most often to Paul to help us define who was in and who was out, what was acceptable, what was questionable, and what was to be flatly rejected. We decided that the head-coverings and no gold jewelry parts were contextual, and we rarely greeted anyone with a holy kiss, but there were still more than enough *do's* and *don'ts* to go around.

Not wanting to make the same mistake the Galatians made,[1] we kept our dealings with the Old Testament brief and at arm's

---

1. Basically, in his letter to the Galatians, Paul rips the church up one side and down the other because they were observing (and presumably requiring

length. The minor prophets were nearly ignored entirely, but the more interesting stories were translated into children's Sunday-school literature. We were familiar with flannel-graph characters depicting accounts that would have given us all nightmares if we had not gotten the censored version.

The Gospels were important, but they, like the Old Testament, described a time before the institution of the church, so they didn't have the same sense of immediate application as the epistles.

Yes, I am completely aware of the multiple layers of irony in those last few paragraphs.

When it came to sermons, Paul's generous use of exhortations, practical directions, and teaching sections provided easy translation into an "introduction, three-points, and conclusion" speech about godly living.

For some of my Christian friends, especially those from mainline and "progressive" traditions (I use quotes because that word is so relative that it is almost meaningless), these descriptions might sound completely alien and ridiculous. For others, they may be painfully familiar.

Again, I don't know your story, but there are scores of people—people I know, respect, and love dearly—for whom this approach to the Bible has long provided a sense of comfort, security, and safety. From preaching to devotional reading, many Christians look to the Bible to give clear-cut answers on what to do in each situation.

For a long time, I wondered if I lacked faith, since I felt neither comfort nor security in this approach. Instead, I felt incredible tension. It seemed like I was forcing myself to pretend the Bible made sense when it just didn't. At the same time, I clung to hope that the Bible made far more sense than any of us realized. Deep down I wondered if our attempts to take the Bible seriously were keeping us from taking it seriously at all.

---

that others observe) Jewish practices, rituals, and laws—actions Paul believed showed a faith in human effort rather than God.

Can you identify with that? Wishing you could reject the Bible and simultaneously longing to discover it? Wanting to both reject and discover faith?

Though things look differently to me now, at the time I was deeply troubled and nervous, and it seemed perfectly reasonable to blame the Apostle Paul. After all, his epistles seemed to be at the root of so many frustrating discussions, positions, and polarizing issues. I found myself edging slowly (or perhaps not so slowly) into my own lopsided treatment of Scripture, where the Gospels served as the climax and resolution, and Acts as the epilogue. Everything after that might as well have been the bibliography in a high school math textbook.

I suspect it will not come as a surprise for you to learn this response didn't ease my tension in the slightest. Despite my best efforts, for several years I simply could not see a viable path forward. Of course, my frustration, which by this time bordered on despair, was not content to remain focused on the Bible. I was beginning to see more clearly, but not in the way I'd hoped. Instead, whole chunks of my faith, my calling, and my life in general were coming into focus, and the image was bleak. I started to see the church as irreparably damaged, but without a legitimate alternative. Being able to declare something as "less than ideal, but manageable" came to symbolize the full extent of my capacity for optimism.

Shaped by, but Not Shackled to, Our Story

Let's face it; there are many things in life over which we have little or no control. We have no choice about when, where, or to whom we are born. We don't control where the hurricane makes landfall, we don't control when the drunk driver will be on the road with us. Though there are certainly things we can do to increase or decrease our chances for longevity, Jesus himself reminded us that worrying about the clock won't add a single hour to our life.

All too often we lack any significant control over what happens to us—and all too often, that sucks. But this is not an argument for fatalism. Instead, on the other side of accepting this reality we discover the groundwork for something much more hope-filled. It turns out there is yet something over which we have total control.

In each situation, regardless of what happens to us—whether miraculous, mundane, or horrific things—we, and no one else, control how we respond to those things.

Both the difficult experiences and the tremendous blessings in our stories shape us, but neither the good nor the bad in our past can ultimately and permanently define who we are—unless we choose to let it. This is true for enormous issues, such as when revolutionaries take a stand against overwhelming forces of oppression or Victor Frankl choosing not to be defined by hatred or despair as a survivor of the Holocaust,[2] and it is also true for less inspiring issues, such as choosing not to be defined by impatience or frustration in a slow-moving grocery check-out line or rush-hour traffic.

Or not being shackled to a lifelong rejection of Paul's letters because of how we've seen them used by others.

What happens if, going back to Hunsberger's four streams, we read Paul's epistles from the perspective of providing the missional paradigm for engaging culture? Remembering that, though we've been invited to do so, we are reading someone else's mail, letters from a teacher to communities striving to work out their calling should be very beneficial. What can we learn about how a missional community discerns its vocation in context? How can we

---

2. If you've never read Victor Frankl's, *Man's Search for Meaning*, I highly recommend it. Originally published in 1959, this firsthand account of the potential for evil and for tremendous resilience that resides within each of us, shows how both extremes can develop out of the choices we make—and describes how the choice to choose our attitude catalyzes change in all other areas. According to Frankl, there is indeed meaning in life itself, and that meaning, "is paralleled by the unconditional value of each and every person... Just as life remains potentially meaningful under any conditions, even those which are most miserable, so too does the value of each and every person stay with him or her" (176). If our value is not derived from our usefulness or some utilitarian contribution, we can then choose how we respond knowing that what happens to us is no more definitive of our worth than what happens because of us.

find ourselves better equipped to engage that discernment process today? Reading from the perspective of a missional community engaged in and committed to the missional direction and purpose of the text might yield some surprising results.

Perhaps your story is very different from my own. Maybe you have never had a problem with Paul, but, instead, simply cannot put up with the violent images of certain sections in the Old Testament. Perhaps you are part of the tiny percentage of people who don't enjoy reading the lists of rules, regulations, and inventories in Leviticus (gasp!). Or maybe your story has predisposed you to distrust people of a certain political party, skin tone, job description, geographic location, or income bracket.

Regardless of the specifics of your story, you can choose whether it will define you. We are *shaped by* our stories, but we are not *shackled to* our stories. Say it out loud: "I am not shackled to my story!"

It has been several years since Paul and I worked out our differences. That reconciliation came about alongside a much broader reclamation in my life, and one of the catalysts can be found here in Philippians with Paul's own version of Wizzywig.

Speaking of Stories.

Philippians is not long, just four chapters, so before we discuss our passage it would be helpful to read the entire letter. We are going to focus specifically on 4:4–9, where Paul gives some parting words that both summarize and conclude the letter. Continue, as we've been doing throughout this book, to read with the four questions of a missional community:

1. What is the missional direction of this letter? Do you notice ways in which this letter continues the trajectory of God's mission in the world?

2. What about the missional purpose? How does this letter form a people who are more equipped to live as the sent people of God?

3. How did the missional identity of the Philippian church impact how the letter was received? What might be heard differently by people who understood themselves as active agents in God's mission versus those who understood their calling to simply believe in God and show up for worship or by those who did not consider themselves believers at all?

4. What about the missional engagement with culture? What principles for connecting with your own community can you find in this letter?

As you read, pay attention to what grabs your attention. If you'd like, write down your reflections and hang on to them. Then go through the same process in a few weeks or months. Comparing our reactions to a passage over time is a good way to glimpse how we're shaped by our current situations and notice the ways in which both our thinking and our ability to listen change over time.

So, seriously, take a few minutes to read Philippians before moving on to the next section.

Snatching Joy from the Jaws of Despair

You don't have to consult a commentary to realize that Paul is in some sort of detainment (jail) as he composes this letter, which makes the hope-filled, often cheerful, tone stand out even more.

Philippians begins, as letters of friendship in the ancient world typically did, with a greeting marked by gratitude and prayer and well-wishing for the recipients. For some reason, Paul's prayer for the church in the early verses of this letter has always caught my attention:

> And this is my prayer: that your love may abound more and more in knowledge and depth of insight, so that you may be able to discern what is best and may be pure and blameless for the day of Christ, filled with the fruit of righteousness that comes through Jesus Christ—to the glory and praise of God.[3]

3. Phil 1:9–11 NIV.

Love abounding in knowledge and depth of insight. Paul says that love is a starting point—and as love increases, so, too, will knowledge and insight, which leads to more capacity to love. Often, we seem to operate as though it were the other way around, don't we? It seems entirely too customary to only love—or even think we can love—that which we know and understand. If the knowledge and depth of insight we gain does not lead to our love abounding more and more, then perhaps we should take a step back and evaluate our mental models.

What would happen if we approached knowledge, not as something to be attained on its own, but as something that results from "love abounding more and more" in our lives?

Following the greeting, Paul begins talking about the negative stuff he's been going through—opposition, imprisonment, persecution . . . you know, the usual. But his focus is very important to note: he describes the ways in which these bad things have led to blessings. His jailers have seen the way in which the story of Jesus impacts a person (and a community) and transforms even their "chains." Other disciples, with Paul's courage and conviction as testimony, have found renewed confidence in God's work in their own lives as well.

He goes on through the rest of what we delineate as chapter 1 describing various scenarios that should be cause for complaint, but are instead put forward as opportunities and blessings.

What is the significance of this? Is this an example of a naïve, pie-in-the-sky detachment from the real world? I don't think so; he clearly seems to recognize both the challenges and potential outcomes they represent.

Should we chalk it up to, "Paul was special and God was doing unusual things in his life?" Well, maybe, but only to the degree that we are willing to say that about ourselves and everyone else.

If it isn't those things, what is it? Let's keep going for now—but keep that question in mind.

Chapter 2 opens with one of my "wait a second" words. Years ago one of my Bible teachers took advantage of every opportunity to remind us, "Whenever we see the word 'therefore,' we need to ask what it's there for."

Yep, it's cheesy. It's also an effective, beneficial, and often needed reminder. Each passage deserves to be read in its context with awareness that it sits within a larger passage. Remember when we discussed the pitfalls of reading Genesis 3 without having reflected on the first two chapters? Failing to maintain the threads of connection greatly increases the likelihood of missing the intended message and replacing it with our own (or someone else's) agenda.

In this case, the word "therefore" introduces the request "if you have any encouragement from being united with Christ . . . then make my joy complete by being like-minded."[4]

From there Paul describes the "attitude" of Jesus (interesting choice of words) as the model for living this life of unity and mutually kenotic (self-emptying) love.

So what is this there for? Well, in the immediately preceding paragraph, the church had been encouraged to view their struggles as a blessing and a sign that the way of Jesus is undercutting the broken and oppressive systems at work in the culture around them. And that encouragement was issued not as a trite platitude, but rather with the weight of someone who was, at that very moment, modeling precisely such a response in the midst of trouble.

And so, with proclamations of gratitude and hope, and exhortations to remain focused on just such things, we come to the "work out your salvation with fear and trembling" section. Given what we've noticed together, this verse sounds very different from the way I've often heard it used.

This isn't an individualistic "ask Jesus into your heart so you can go to heaven when you die" statement. It is a challenge for the whole community together to pursue the way, the attitude, and the mission of Jesus together in any situation.

Then we come to chapter 3 and again Paul encourages the church to rejoice, even under the pressure of opposition. He takes a different approach this time, and speaks to the inadequacy of their opponents' arguments and posturing.

---

4. Phil 2:1–2 NIV.

Philippians 4:4–9: Think about Such Things

This sounds a lot like a pep talk to those being bombarded with stump speeches, rhetoric, and negative campaign ads. From the reading, it isn't clear just how dire the situation for the church in Philippi was (though, if we wanted to get all nerdy with the historical context, we could). In any case, it seems pretty obvious that this letter is meant, at least in part, to help this community maintain momentum in the face of significant difficulty.

That brings us to the focus of this discussion, and circles all the way back to Wizzywig. You didn't think I'd forgotten about our old friend, did you?

Chapter 4 begins with another "therefore" and calls the church to "stand firm in the Lord in this way."[5]

In what way? In the way that entire letter up to this point has been describing: the way of a life marked by rejoicing in all situations, loving one another, and embracing discipleship in the way of Jesus!

Not sure that's the point? Apparently, Paul anticipated your reticence, because he repeats, "Rejoice in the Lord always. I will say it again: Rejoice!" Amid these trials, by keeping focused on what truly matters and continuing to approach God with thankfulness, "the peace of God, which transcends understanding, will guard your hearts and your minds in Christ Jesus."[6]

That leads us to verse 8 and another important word—finally. This is the word that always caught my attention as a kid during the sermon, whether I was awake or not, because it meant that we were almost done. It's the word that signifies the crescendo, the finale, the tying-it-all-together moment.

> Finally, brother and sisters, whatever is true, whatever is noble, whatever is right, whatever is pure, whatever is lovely, whatever is admirable—if anything is excellent or praiseworthy—think about such things.[7]

---

5. Phil 4:1 NIV.
6. Phil 4:4, 7 NIV.
7. Phil 4:8 NIV.

For years, I heard this verse mostly as an accusation against those who were doing otherwise. But now, particularly considering what we've discussed here, I think that understanding defeats the purpose, and the actual purpose defeats the paradigm of that (mis)understanding.

Paul says to us, "What you see is what you get." Only this time it means more than "you can take this at face value." It means that what we see, what we focus on, what we think about, is the very thing we're most likely to discover.

If we are obsessed with fault-finding, we will always find faults. If we are looking for a fight, we'll find one—or twenty. If we're constantly obsessing about failure, worst-case scenario, why something won't work, what others will say and do, all the things that can go wrong . . . they will. That is, if we get around to trying anything at all.

I've upset several of my friends by suggesting this is a major flaw in many popular books, curriculums, and programs for "men's group" accountability. These groups, particularly in North American Evangelical contexts, are very often focused almost exclusively on lust—and its various ramifications, symptoms, and outcomes.

For the sake of argument, I'm willing to temporarily set aside the notion that perhaps there are more things for men to address in their life than just sex. (Crazy notion, I know.) The bigger issue, from what I can see, is that focusing constantly on how many times we've had impure thoughts is like asking alcoholics to meditate on the experiences that entice them to drink. It is nothing more than a setup for the next failure.

It also assumes that the goal is to not look at a woman with lust—which often seems to mean, don't look at woman who isn't your spouse. This doesn't really get us anywhere though. Nothing in this mindset will ever equip us to look at someone, man or woman, and see them as God sees them—as a unique, beloved person. Instead we've simply gone from viewing others as an object to be coveted to treating them as an object to be avoided . . . but they are still an object. By focusing on the shortcoming, what we see is what we get. What we look for is what we find. What we obsess about is what we become.

If our entire belief system is structured around sin management, then what is it that we are going to be thinking about most often? Sin. That's just one reason the approach doesn't accomplish anything close to the amazing transformations we read about in Acts or those that have been witnessed in exponential movements throughout history. It is never sufficient to define your calling in terms of what you're against. Those who find themselves amid movements and moments that transcend the status quo are likely those who remain singularly focused on that to which they have been called: that which they long for most deeply.

To be the sent people of God is always going to mean entering the dark places. Sometimes that darkness descends in the form of direct persecution, and other times it is willingly embraced in solidarity with others who are marginalized and oppressed. In either situation, by keeping the preferred future in mind, by "forgetting what is behind, and straining toward what is ahead"[8] we discover that the world no longer looks the same. Instead of seeing problems and the potential for failure, we see opportunities and the potential for greater discovery.

G. K. Chesterton said, "An adventure is only an inconvenience rightly considered. An inconvenience is an adventure wrongly considered."[9] I don't know if he meant to paraphrase Paul, but he did it brilliantly. When we read Philippians as a missional community of disciples, we are reminded that while we are shaped by our particular stories, we are not shackled to them.

We learn that the things we avoid or overcome do not determine our faith or lack of faith. Instead, by consistently choosing love, our knowledge and depth of insight abound more and more. By embracing a posture of gratitude and thanksgiving, regardless of trials we face, we begin to see things in a whole new light.

---

8. Phil 3:13 NIV.
9. Chesterton, *On Chasing After One's Hat*, 6.

WHAT KIND OF GOD?

We begin to see opportunity. We see reason to hope. We see the kingdom of God breaking in all around us, and we see ways in which we are invited to participate.

What we see is what we get.

... So, what do we see?

Notes from Denise

This passage of Scripture has always been a personal favorite of mine, so I paid extra attention to how it fits into the Story.

I am reminded here that I, and only I—hopefully with my attention tuned to God's grace abounding—can choose how I react to things.

I can choose to view things through a lens that is tyrannical and judgmental, or I can choose to pay attention to where the Story is taking us.

I can choose to understand that things said in a specific way and specific context must be understood that way and that I can—and must—do the hard work of finding the thread of the Story underneath.

I can recognize that underneath the language of another context, the Love continues to flow. That flow is life-giving as the Community continues to pour out and out and out. I can breathe easier in the bone-deep perception of the peace and joy so vast that we can grab hold of it when our own smaller story threatens to shackle us.

And then what if, to avoid those shackles, we embrace the idea that "What we look for is what we find. What we obsess about is what we become." If so, we could simply choose to look for the love and the peace and the joy and obsess about those things. Why wouldn't we?

6

Revelation 21:1—22:5: Now Among the People

THE FIRST THING I noticed was his stooped posture and shuffling gait. His skin, a canvas of deep wrinkles and liver spots, combined with ill-fitting, decades-old clothing to create an image of feebleness and frailty. And he was bearing down on me with the determination it takes to get through eighty years of life.

Even before he spoke, I began to suspect that those initial visual cues might be misleading. I noticed his air of confidence and the determined set to his jaw. This was not the face of someone shrouded in a haze of confusion. His eyes also refused to join the ruse. They were bright, intelligent, and . . . there was something else there . . .

"*Do you know what your problem is?*"

Ah, yes, cantankerousness. Totally should have seen that coming. Not knowing what else to say, I laughed and replied, "You mean you've already narrowed it down to one?" Judging from his response, it is possible he didn't hear me, though I suspect he just chose to ignore my attempt at levity.

"*You've lost the simplicity of the gospel.*"

I had just finished teaching the first in a series of classes on Wednesday nights at our church. The series was called, "How to Read the Bible," and it was intended to deal with some of the same questions we have been addressing in this book. I hoped, over the course of ten weeks, to provide a general overview of the Bible in terms of genres, historical background, issues with language and translation, and the importance of keeping specific passages or verses situated within their larger context.

One person, at least, found the topic less than compelling.

For my new friend (and, yes, over time I developed a genuine fondness for him, though I could never tell for sure whether he'd made up his mind one way or the other about me), my "problem" was simple—I was making things too complicated.

His pronouncement seemed at once accusation and diagnosis. Though his tone certainly seemed confrontational and more than a little condescending, it did not seem hostile so much as a matter-of-fact assessment. To be honest, this particular blend tends to push my buttons more than angry insults or intentionally personal attacks.

However, in this case I didn't get upset. Ironically, the very things I'd been discussing in the class—the same content that inspired this interaction—played a direct role in helping me avoid defensiveness.

First, I recognized the genre of our exchange—specifically, the "Eighty-Plus-Years-of-Life, Say-What-I-Want-to-a-Whipper-Snapper" prerogative. Much of my life has been spent around old ranchers and other "crusty" types. I am not only familiar with this prerogative, to a certain degree, I respect it—and, if I'm completely honest, I look forward to a day when I have earned it for myself.

Secondly, I understood the historical context behind his comment. Far from being caught off guard by his strong resistance, I was both surprised and a little disappointed that it had not surfaced during the class itself. It is difficult to address and constructively respond to resistance when it remains unvoiced. The tendency to reject, deny, or downplay the importance of genre, language, and context is a common (and unfortunate) position that can be traced back to the founding principles of our congregation's faith tradition.

Revelation 21:1—22:5: Now Among the People

The Churches of Christ, along with the Disciples of Christ and Independent Christian Churches, are part of the Stone-Campbell Restoration Movement, which began during the early nineteenth-century American revival movement known as "The Second Great Awakening."

The early leaders of the movement were frustrated and disillusioned by matters they believed were inconsistent with Christian unity and that too closely resembled the oppressive religious systems so prevalent in Europe. They challenged the divide between clergy and laity that was so marked in traditional Christian churches and emphasized common people's ability—and responsibility—to read, understand, and follow the Bible without control from priests or clergy. They disagreed with the inherent divisiveness in the proliferation of Protestant denominations, each with their own creeds, covenants, rules, and membership vows.

Largely independent of one another, various groups within what would become the Stone-Campbell Restoration Movement sought to restore unity to the church by seeking a "simple pattern of New Testament Christianity" without requiring additional creedal statements or extra-biblical complexities.

What began as a belief that lay people had the ability to read and understand the Bible soon developed into pockets of anti-intellectualism and suspicious distrust of formal theological education.[1]

Knowing this historical context has not magically shielded me from frustration when I encounter this mindset. It has, however, helped me understand why I encounter it so frequently.

A contextually informed reading of the Bible is not an indicator that one has "lost the simplicity of the gospel." Instead, I would suggest that it helps guard against a *simplistic* approach to reading that can be inadvertently skewed by accumulated cultural trappings and assumptions.

---

1. For more thorough accounts of the Stone-Campbell Restoration Movement, see Hughes, *Reviving the Ancient Faith*; Foster et al., *The Encyclopedia of the Stone-Campbell Movement*.

WHAT KIND OF GOD?

The concept of a "simple gospel" can itself be a bit misleading. Perhaps instead of simple, as Alan Hirsch suggests about the *Jesus is Lord* confession, a better descriptor might be "simplex." It is, at the same time, simple and complex: "Simple in that it can be easily understood and passed on from person to person; complex, because it carries the full weight of biblical monotheism."[2]

In one sense, yes, the gospel (or "good news") is simple: the kingdom of God is at hand, and we are all invited to participate in that kingdom.[3] And yet, what precisely did Jesus mean when he said that the kingdom is at hand? It seems that much of the New Testament was focused on answering that question to one degree or another. And what does it mean that we are all invited to participate in that kingdom? Even though God gave Peter a graphic lesson on this topic,[4] he apparently continued to struggle with its implications—enough so that Paul felt compelled to confront his inconsistency.[5]

Even if the gospel is simple, it is not hard to imagine ways that we can confuse or complicate the message. We can add any number of modifiers, disclaimers, prerequisites, and addendums. Perhaps we expound, refine, expand, or contract in response to perceived abuses or to provide clarification. Maybe we adapt to culture or feel the need to stand against adaptations that might

---

2. Hirsch and Ferguson, *On the Verge*, 125.

3. Mark 1:14–15 NRSV. "Jesus came to Galilee, proclaiming the good news of God, and saying, 'The time is fulfilled, and the kingdom of God has come near; repent, and believe in the good news.'"

4. Acts 10. God uses a vision of foods that were traditionally held as unclean for Jewish people to show Peter that the gospel is for all people, including those the Jews considered unclean.

5. Gal 2:11–14, NRSV. "But when Cephas [Peter] came to Antioch, I opposed him to his face, because he stood self-condemned; for until certain people came from James, he used to eat with the Gentiles. But after they came, he drew back and kept himself separate for fear of the circumcision faction. And the other Jews joined him in this hypocrisy, so that even Barnabas was led astray by their hypocrisy. But when I saw that they were not acting consistently with the truth of the gospel, I said to Cephas before them all, 'If you, though a Jew, live like a Gentile and not like a Jew, how can you compel the Gentiles to live like Jews?'"

lead to syncretism. Over time, as new people and new generations come along, the origin of these adaptations begins to fade. Eventually the "why" is forgotten, even while the "what" persists. And that can create some decidedly not-simple situations.

We are more likely to lose the simplicity of the gospel through a lack of contextual awareness than through its pursuit.

I once heard a story about a small country church with a peculiar tradition. Each Sunday the communion elements would be placed under a fine cloth at the front of the sanctuary. When it came time to celebrate the Eucharist, men would come forward, solemnly lift the cloth, carefully fold it, and place it beneath the altar.

For the members of this congregation, the practice was familiar and venerated. For the church's new preacher, on the other hand, the practice seemed odd and needlessly time-consuming. Sharing this observation, he suggested that they simply stop using the cloth. No one could explain precisely why the elements were covered and then ritualistically uncovered in this way, other than that it emphasized the sacred and mysterious nature of the Lord's Supper. The mere suggestion that they stop the practice was taken as an affront bordering on sacrilege.

The young preacher was intrigued by their strict adherence to a seemingly random ritual (which proves that this preacher was, in fact, quite young). He began digging through the church records and interviewing everyone he could, hoping to discover the origin of the Communion Cloth. His search remained fruitless until, at last, he spoke with one of the oldest members of the congregation; one who was just a small child when the congregation was founded. (One might wonder why this wasn't the first person he asked, but that isn't how these stories work, is it?)

As it turns out, the answer was as simple and pragmatic as it was anticlimactic. Before the church building was constructed, the congregation met outside, under the shade of a large oak tree. It didn't take them long to get tired of dealing with falling leaves, bird droppings, and flies on the bread and wine, so they covered them with a sheet. There was no mystery or sacred symbolism involved, just a common-sense, pragmatic solution to an ordinary inconvenience.

I don't know how the congregation responded once they rediscovered this little tidbit of their own history. Maybe they decided it was okay to stop covering the elements. Maybe they continued the practice as a reminder of their roots. Or maybe they decided that, whatever the original purpose, covering the elements had become an important way to communicate their community's value on the sacred and mysterious nature of the Eucharist. Whatever they decided, they were finally equipped to approach that decision with intentionality and clarity.

Story has a way of pulling—perhaps even dragging—us out of uninformed simplicity and into complexity. There is no doubt that the complexity can be disorienting and even frightening; however, if we choose to remain in the story there is often a more vivid, robust, and deep simplicity to be discovered on the other side, or perhaps right in the midst, of that complexity.

Even a cursory glance should be enough to tell us that there is already a great deal of complexity in the contemporary landscape of Christianity, and that complexity only deepens when we consider the past two thousand years of church history.

One of the most interesting aspects of my experiences in church planting has been the simple act of reading the Bible with a community that combines just a little of that complexity and diversity.

When there are people in one room who come from Catholic, mainline Protestant, charismatic, and a broad spectrum of evangelical contexts, the conversation is rarely boring. Things get even more interesting when you add in those who have no previous connection to a formal faith community of any kind along with some who were raised in a different religion altogether.

As we read the Bible together we discover that there are passages and books that are largely ignored in some traditions yet foundational and formative in others. That isn't to say there aren't points of overlap or similarity. Even in diverse contexts, an invitation to study Leviticus will often induce grimaces of displeasure

Revelation 21:1—22:5: Now Among the People

among those who are at least somewhat familiar with the Bible. Inviting them to study Song of Songs (Song of Solomon) elicits giggles and awkward fidgeting—particularly from males between the ages of thirteen and sixty-three. Unless the room is filled with Old Testament scholars, the suggestion to study Nahum or Zephaniah will often be met with blank stares.

And though it isn't always the case, inviting people to study Revelation can easily result in raised eyebrows and attempts to change the subject.

Like with the ritual of the Communion Cloth, reading Revelation without understanding the context and genre can be time-consuming, confusing, and fraught with accumulated misunderstandings. That does not mean that applying a little context will suddenly transform Revelation into an "easy read." Even with a better awareness of the context and genre, we may still find the passage hard to understand, and we may still be uncomfortable as we read, because this is one of those stories that will quickly drag us right into the midst of complexity.

Like many of the writings in Scripture, Revelation doesn't conform completely to one genre or style. There are elements of a letter of instruction, as well as sections of prophecy.[6] However, the major writing style used in this book is *apocalyptic*—which makes sense considering that the Greek word *apokalypsis* means "uncovering" or "revelation." This style of writing was easily recognizable to the recipients.[7]

There are three characteristics that will be helpful to keep in mind as we read.[8] First, apocalyptic literature, unlike forms such as prophecy, was truly a literary work. In other words, they did

---

6. If you're looking for an excellent and accessible overview/introduction of genres and themes in the Bible, I highly recommend two works by Gordon D. Fee and Douglas Stuart: *How to Read the Bible for All Its Worth* (4th ed.) and its companion, *How to Read the Bible Book by Book: A Guided Tour*.

7. See Koester, *Revelation*, 27–30.

8. These three aspects are not meant to be exhaustive, but are representative and helpful for us in our current discussion. See Fee and Stuart, *How to Read the Bible for All Its Worth*, 249–64, for further description of these and other aspects of apocalyptic literature.

not begin as oral tradition, nor were they transcribed on the fly. Instead, these documents were formally and carefully stylized with symbolic imagery, numerical groupings, and detailed word pictures to draw on the power of imagination to connect with the visceral elements of the story. This is not unlike the way that parables, fables, and even creative anecdotes function.

The second characteristic we'll notice is the tendency to draw specifically on mythology and the realm of fantasy. Descriptions of dragons and other mythical beasts invite the hearer into a narrative of cosmic proportions. By using such non-literal imagery, apocalyptic literature is also able to speak truth and denounce forces of oppression in situations where doing so openly could be hazardous for both writer and recipient.

Writing about this complex situation, Brian McLaren described it in this way:

> The original readers of Revelation lived in constant threat of religious oppression from the religious authorities and the Roman Empire. In that environment, you can't speak—and certainly can't write—a word of criticism against the government and other authorities; if you are caught with such subversive literature in your possession, you'll be imprisoned, maybe killed. But if you don't speak or write about your oppression, your oppressors have succeeded in controlling you, silencing you, intimidating you.... Here's what you do: you tell the truth about those in power—that they're corrupt, bloodthirsty, and doomed—but you do so covertly.... In this way, you refuse to be silenced in fear—and you don't create incriminating evidence that could lead to torture and death for the author and readers of the literature.[9]

That leads us to the third important characteristic. Though greatly varied in style, content, format, and purpose, apocalyptic works often develop out of communities suffering tremendous persecution, oppression, and enslavement.

---

9. McLaren, *Secret Message of Jesus*, 176.

Revelation 21:1—22:5: Now Among the People

Not surprisingly, the themes of judgment, redemption, and hope for salvation are very common. In the face of unspeakable oppression, the psalmist gives voice to the people's cry in Psalm 79:

> How long, Lord? Will you be angry forever?
> How long will your jealousy burn like fire?
> Pour out your wrath on the nations
> that do not acknowledge you,
> on the kingdoms
> that do not call on your name;
> for they have devoured Jacob
> and devastated his homeland.[10]

For some of us, these words are like nails on the chalkboard. Truly, this is not the cry of the comfortable, or even the mildly inconvenienced—it is undeniably the literature of the oppressed. For people, such as myself, who have very little experience being truly oppressed, it is essential to keep that distinction in mind.

I realize that someday I will die, but in my mind that day still resides in a relatively distant future. So, I do not have the same connection to songs about the "sweet by and by" that bring such comfort to my grandparents and older friends approaching the end of their life on earth. The same is true when I consider songs and sermons that arose from the experience of slaves in North America. It is all too easy to apply my own contextual lens and evaluate these stories from a distance.

My best hope for true understanding comes when I can sit with someone experiencing oppression and listen to his or her story. That isn't always possible, and, even when it is, I am faced with the realization that I can only see in part.

But my struggle to see more clearly reminds me of the hope that a day is coming when we will all see one another with true clarity. And in that moment of hope I find solidarity with all those who long for the day when God will, finally and fully, bring completion to the mission of reconciliation.

---

10. Ps 79:5–7 NIV.

WHAT KIND OF GOD?

And it just so happens that Revelation 21:1–5 describes precisely such a day.

> Then I saw "a new heaven and a new earth," for the first heaven and the first earth had passed away, and there was no longer any sea. I saw the Holy City, the new Jerusalem, coming down out of heaven from God, prepared as a bride beautifully dressed for her husband. And I heard a loud voice from the throne saying, "Look! God's dwelling place is now among the people, and he will dwell with them. They will be his people, and God himself will be with them and be their God. 'He will wipe every tear from their eyes. There will be no more death' or mourning or crying or pain, for the old order of things has passed away."
>
> He who was seated on the throne said, "I am making everything new!" Then he said, "Write this down, for these words are trustworthy and true."[11]

As with all journeys, we began our exploration of the Bible's narrative "in the beginning." We encountered poetry describing God as wholly different—as one who speaks universes into existence and hovers over the chaos. And yet we watched as this God stepped into the midst of it all, walked in the garden, and formed beloved children from the soil. We saw that the garden was not a random location, but was carefully and intentionally created to host the shared life between Creator and Creation. We marveled at the barely mentioned but tantalizingly mysterious tree of life, which stood in the middle of the garden with its equally magical sibling. As we learned the nature of that sibling—the tree of knowledge of good and evil—we couldn't help but wonder why such a tree was ever planted.

Our discussion was focused on the creation stories and the activities of the Creator. For that reason, we intentionally stopped short of reading Genesis 3. We introduced a pause: a purposeful cessation of progress. This detour from our tendency to rush

---

11. Rev 21:1–5 NIV.

ahead also reminded us to define the story in terms of God's actions rather than humanity's.

Yet, if we turn back to those pages, we know what we would find. We know that the next chapter of the story bore witness to one tree fading into the background as the other tree took center stage in the narrative.

We would mourn with the Creator as the children chose fruit from the tree of death over the tree of life. And to the extent we were able to enter the story, we might wonder just how this God could ever fulfill God's promises of restoration and reconciliation.

Since that first discussion, we have traveled, in rapid fashion, across landscapes and centuries. We moved through periods of slavery and prosperity, faithfulness and betrayal, confusion and clarity, hope and despair. Throughout it all we have seen certain trends remain constant. God is the one who is able to hover above the chaos and the one for whom the entire cosmos serves as throne room. At the same time, we consistently discover this God coming near, dwelling in a tent among the people, and expressing undying love for people who struggle to comprehend what such a statement even means.

All along we've noted an overall trajectory to the story. We have stopped to notice both the missional direction and purpose of this story. Should it then come as a surprise that the story concludes with a proclamation that God will dwell among the people?

Take a moment to reread the first five verses of chapter 21. Allow the words to simmer. Listen carefully, and attend to them.

As you read, what do you notice? What stands out? Remembering all that has come before, what do you notice about the missional direction and purpose of our narrative? Before you continue reading, take a moment to at least consider, and perhaps write down, your reflections.

For years, though I read it many times, I was unable to actually *see* this passage. My imagination had been shaped thoroughly by a framework of extraction. In my mind the culmination of history would involve the destruction of Earth, while every person who had ever lived would be drawn away into God's presence for judgment.

We see a very different picture in this vision. In an utterly consistent, yet often overlooked move, it is God who comes near ... yet again. The God who planted a garden for humanity, the God who dwelled among the people in Exodus,[12] the God who dwelled among us in the person of Jesus,[13] is once more choosing to dwell right in the midst of the people. To those who are listening, this word, *dwell*, is yelling, at full volume, "this is where everything has been heading!" This is a vision of God's mission fulfilled. All things are being made new, including the experience of shared life in the Community of Love.

This was the original intention in Genesis, and we know how that ended. So, what is to keep history from repeating itself? The rest of chapter 21 addresses that question, though it may not do so in the way we would prefer.

It will be helpful, as much as we are able, to consider this passage from the perspective and context of an oppressed people. Early church tradition and the majority of contemporary scholars date this letter at around AD 95.[14] If that is correct, then the original recipients either remembered firsthand or grew up in the immediate aftermath of Rome utterly destroying Jerusalem in AD 70. Imagine that an empire and its army have occupied your land, desolated your most sacred spaces, demanded complete loyalty to its emperor, and even now threaten to extinguish what little remains of your life.

If you were among those recipients, what then might you hear in this passage?

---

12. Exod 29:45–46: "I will dwell among the Israelites, and I will be their God. And they shall know that I am the Lord their God, who brought them out of the land of Egypt that I might dwell among them; I am the Lord their God."

13. John 1:14a: "The Word became flesh and made his dwelling among us."

14. Though some scholars have suggested an earlier date around AD 68–69, the majority opinion holding to the later date can be traced all the way back to Irenaeus in the second-century. See Reid, *IVP Dictionary*, s.v. "Revelation, Book of."

He said to me: "It is done. I am the Alpha and the Omega, the Beginning and the End. To the thirsty I will give water without cost from the spring of the water of life. Those who are victorious will inherit all this, and I will be their God and they will be my children. But the cowardly, the unbelieving, the vile, the murderers, the sexually immoral, those who practice magic arts, the idolaters and all liars—they will be consigned to the fiery lake of burning sulfur. This is the second death."

One of the seven angels who had the seven bowls full of the seven last plagues came and said to me, "Come, I will show you the bride, the wife of the Lamb." And he carried me away in the Spirit to a mountain great and high, and showed me the Holy City, Jerusalem, coming down out of heaven from God. It shone with the glory of God, and its brilliance was like that of a very precious jewel, like a jasper, clear as crystal. It had a great, high wall with twelve gates, and with twelve angels at the gates. On the gates were written the names of the twelve tribes of Israel. There were three gates on the east, three on the north, three on the south and three on the west. The wall of the city had twelve foundations, and on them were the names of the twelve apostles of the Lamb.

The angel who talked with me had a measuring rod of gold to measure the city, its gates and its walls. The city was laid out like a square, as long as it was wide. He measured the city with the rod and found it to be 12,000 stadia in length, and as wide and high as it is long. The angel measured the wall using human measurement, and it was 144 cubits thick. The wall was made of jasper, and the city of pure gold, as pure as glass. The foundations of the city walls were decorated with every kind of precious stone. The first foundation was jasper, the second sapphire, the third agate, the fourth emerald, the fifth onyx, the sixth ruby, the seventh chrysolite, the eighth beryl, the ninth topaz, the tenth turquoise, the eleventh jacinth, and the twelfth amethyst. The twelve gates were twelve pearls, each gate made of a single pearl. The great street of the city was of gold, as pure as transparent glass.

I did not see a temple in the city, because the Lord God Almighty and the Lamb are its temple. The city

> does not need the sun or the moon to shine on it, for the glory of God gives it light, and the Lamb is its lamp. The nations will walk by its light, and the kings of the earth will bring their splendor into it. On no day will its gates ever be shut, for there will be no night there. The glory and honor of the nations will be brought into it. Nothing impure will ever enter it, nor will anyone who does what is shameful or deceitful, but only those whose names are written in the Lamb's book of life.[15]

If we were sitting face to face right now, I would be silent. I would ask for your reactions, reflections, and response. Obviously, we are not sitting face to face, and it is equally obvious (to those who know me) that I am completely unskilled in the practice of omniscience. So, even though I will never know your response unless you write to me and tell me, I encourage you to take a few moments to reflect on and, perhaps, write down your reaction to this passage.

What similarities or differences do you notice between your own reaction to this passage and how you might expect an oppressed people to react? What insights can you gain from those points of overlap and divergence?

With these reflections in mind, including those from the opening verses of chapter 21, let's continue to the next section in chapter 22:1–5.

> Then the angel showed me the river of the water of life, as clear as crystal, flowing from the throne of God and of the Lamb down the middle of the great street of the city. On each side of the river stood the tree of life, bearing twelve crops of fruit, yielding its fruit every month. And the leaves of the tree are for the healing of the nations. No longer will there be any curse. The throne of God and of the Lamb will be in the city, and his servants will serve him. They will see his face, and his name will be on their foreheads. There will be no more night. They will not need the light of a lamp or the light of the sun, for

---

15. Rev 21:6–27 NIV.

the Lord God will give them light. And they will reign forever and ever.¹⁶

The tree of knowledge of good and evil may have taken the stage first, but where is it now? It has itself faded into obscurity. In this vision of culmination, the tree of death is no more, and the tree of life is once more in the center of the community. In fact, the tree of life stands on either side of the river of the water of life, which flows from the throne of God down the center of Main Street! Its leaves are for the healing of the nations, and the curse (another sign pointing back to Genesis) is no more.

Eden has not simply been recovered. Like all things, Eden has been made new. Though the scenery has changed, we end our story where it began: a carefully and intentionally created space, amid God's good creation, where Creator and Creation will dwell together in a true experience of community.

This is precisely what Christopher Wright was referring to when he said, "Within this story, as narrated or anticipated by the Bible, there is at work the God whose mission is evident from creation to new creation . . . This is the story of God's mission."¹⁷

All the ups and downs we encounter throughout the Bible are bookended by the same image. Genesis 1–2 and Revelation 21–22 both feature God's deep love for creation and commitment to creating space—literally and figuratively—for humanity to experience true community within the Community of Love. These passages provide a framework for interpreting the missional direction and purpose of the biblical narrative both individually and corporately.

Behold! The God who speaks universes into being has moved into the neighborhood and is making all things new! What does it mean to join in God's mission? Look out your window. What is God already doing right here? Run out and ask if you can help.

---

16. Rev 22:1–5 NIV.
17. Wright, *Mission of God*, 47.

WHAT KIND OF GOD?

Notes from Denise

And so we come full circle...

The created once more can draw close to the Tree of Life as God comes near yet again to embrace creation. The Community of Love overflows its banks as the relentless trajectory of the history of the mission of God—Father, Son, and Holy Spirit—and the purpose to restore and redeem all of creation to its intended state is fulfilled. Again, all are in community. And indeed, it is *very good*.

7

Little Children and One Fat Ox

From the Mouths of Babes

Though it had yet to reach the hottest part of the day, the cicadas were already filling the air with their racket as the Sunday afternoon temperatures pushed closer to the century mark. Two men walked with me around the property of a large, eclectic looking house in Fort Worth, Texas. A sign near the front door named this the Phoebe Palmer House in honor of the nineteenth-century Methodist known for her leadership in the Holiness Movement and, too rarely, for her role as a somewhat enigmatic but deeply influential Christian mystic.[1]

The Palmer House was part of the Missional Wisdom Foundation's Epworth Project, and it was also part of the reason these men had flown to Texas from Alaska. Both were participating in our two-year program that trains and coaches people to launch and lead missional communities. They had already been with us for several days, having attended a Christian community development conference, and were wrapping up with a few opportunities to see first-hand the sort of work we talked about in our training.

---

1. See Heath, *Naked Faith*.

WHAT KIND OF GOD?

The Phoebe Palmer House was an interesting example with its homemade prayer labyrinth and community garden in the back yard and an assortment of supplies in the house for an art-therapy class that several of the women were leading. However, at that particular moment, both men were more interested in discussing what we had experienced immediately prior to visiting the Palmer House.

They had arrived at my own house that morning a little before ten to join in worship with The Gathering—a missional community that typically meets in our living room. On that particular Sunday, the house was pretty full. With four young families (including eight children under the age of ten), an older couple nearing retirement age, and our two extremely-far-from-home visitors, calling the living room "cozy" would have been a stretch.

After everyone had eaten their fill of the haphazard, but always abundant, assortment of food, it was the ten-year-old's turn to lead us in the morning's liturgy from *Common Prayer: A Liturgy for Ordinary Radicals*.[2] Those who didn't have a copy of the book were encouraged to follow along on the television screen.

We sang a random assortment of songs together. A few were old traditional hymns, just as many were children's songs (including one that the, only recently talking, preschool-age girl would lead for us every week). Some included a haltingly strummed guitar, others were sung a cappella, and the two "repeat after me" songs were accompanied only by a djembe (those were requested nearly every week by one or more of the elementary-age boys).

During the time set aside to "offer prayers for others," young and old alike shared requests for friends who were sick, a family going through difficult times, and traveling mercies for those who were away from home—including our friends from the Frozen North. Each request, whether offered by a sixty-year-old or a six-year-old, was concluded with "Lord in your mercy" and followed by a chorus of "Hear our prayers."

Rather than the suggested Scripture reading, our community was in the process of reading through Exodus at the time, so we

---

2. Claiborne, Wilson-Hartgrove, and Okoro, *Common Prayer*

spent about half an hour reading and discussing the text for that week. After the discussion, my eight-year-old son joined me as we prayed over the Communion elements (the bread was taken directly from our brunch and the cup was filled with plain old grape juice from the refrigerator). I held the cup, my son held the bread. As he broke pieces off, handing them to each person in turn, he said, "This is Jesus's body that gives life." I followed by offering the cup and saying, "This is Jesus's blood that saves life."

After the remaining sections of prayer and reading, the ten-year-old began the blessing that marks the end of our worship gathering each week. Everyone joined in, the words comforting and familiar:

> May the peace of the Lord Christ go with you: wherever he may send you;
>> May he guide you through the wilderness: protect you through the storm;
>> May he bring you home rejoicing: at the wonders he has shown you;
>> May he bring you home rejoicing: once again into our doors.[3]

Though there were still people at the house, the Alaskan pilgrims and I departed around 12:30 to visit the Palmer House before they headed to the airport for their return flight.

As we walked around, the guys commented on the beauty of such simple worship—including the ways that the worship combined a structured liturgy with informal and seemingly spur-of-the-moment elements—and with all ages participating together in every aspect. One commented on the power of hearing the liturgy read by a child and the tears that filled his eyes when that small voice offered him "Jesus's body that gives life." The other mentioned how he wished his congregation could experience the deep and insightful conversation around the Bible reading. I was momentarily confused when he made the (somewhat offhand) comment that it

---

3. Claiborne, Wilson-Hartgrove, and Okoro, *Common Prayer*. This blessing is used to conclude the morning prayers in *Common Prayer*.

was probably easier to do this sort of worship and discussion with so many seminary students and clergy in such a small gathering.

When his words finally registered, I interrupted him to clarify that, actually, I was the only one in our community who had been to seminary.

Both sets of eyes turned to me with disbelief. "What? How is that even possible?"

"What you just experienced," I explained to them, "is one of the main reasons we feel so strongly about the importance of missional community."

Identifying as a "sent community" impacts more than just service and presence in the community. It also transforms the way we view worship, ministry, discipleship, and, yes, even the way we read and discuss the Bible. We are all in this together . . . even the kids. The whole church exists as the sent people of God, and the Bible belongs to the whole church; it belongs to the community, not just the clergy. The first time you come face-to-face with what is undeniably the wisdom of the Holy Spirit spoken from the mouth of a child, it becomes pretty easy to lay down any remaining preconceptions about who has enough training or education to participate in the conversation—regardless of which side of that training you may find yourself.

We all bring different gifts to the table. My training in theology and biblical studies is certainly one of those gifts, but it is only one of many gifts represented in our community. I am often amazed at the insights others are able to offer; aspects and perspectives I might never have considered. My gifts strengthen our community, and I certainly hope that contribution is valuable, but if my voice were the only one being heard, that would be an unthinkable travesty.

This collaborative and participatory experience is a great blessing rooted in the core identity of a missional community. That doesn't mean that it is unique to missional communities, or that it will be immediately natural for those who develop a missional mindset. We are not striving to create something novel. Jonathan Wilson-Hartgrove illustrates this same principle when he draws from Peter Maurin's description of the Catholic Worker movement as "a vision so old, it looks new." He notes that, "We can be encouraged by signs of something new precisely because they're signs of what God has been doing for centuries . . . [there's] no reason to think that God is doing something in our midst that hasn't been done before."[4]

Many of the core assumptions found in a missional mindset are present, not only across the ages, but across contexts. A great spectrum of experience exists among the many different denominations, faith traditions, and even regional cultural influences. Generally, one might expect to see more of an egalitarian approach (at least in clergy-laity dynamics) among the various Free Church traditions than in more liturgical mainline contexts. Not surprisingly, a tremendous range of diverse expectations is also present among specific congregations, groups, and certainly individual people in any one of those settings, regardless of the predominant culture in which they function.

Our experiences in teaching and presenting a missional paradigm have elicited a wide spectrum of responses. There are those for whom these ideas represent a disorienting and radical shift in thought. On the other hand, it isn't uncommon to get a very different response from people situated in or shaped by more community-oriented cultures. On those occasions our words may even receive blank stares, as though the listeners are waiting for us to get past the introduction and say something "new." But overall, perhaps the most common response has been, "Yes! I have been longing for this! I just didn't have an intentional and consistent framework to describe it."

Though it may be new to some, there is nothing truly novel about approaching the Bible "from the assumption that the whole Bible renders to us the story of God's mission through God's people in their engagement with God's world for the sake of the whole of God's creation."[5] We are not trying to come up with something

---

4. Wilson-Hartgrove, *New Monasticism*, 41.
5. Wright, *Mission of God*, 51.

new to be more relevant; we're reclaiming something ancient to be more present.

How Much Does That Ox Weigh?

A missional hermeneutic, conscious of the direction and purpose of the story, our identity as readers, and implications for engaging culture, is always going to be experienced most fully when approached and applied in community. The community's importance is rooted in a Trinitarian theology, and its validity has even been attested to in social science.

In his book *The Wisdom of Crowds*, James Suroweicki recounts a now famous experiment that uncovered an unexpected, and somewhat mind-boggling, wealth of wisdom present in a presumably ignorant crowd of individuals. In 1906 a British scientist named Francis Galton traveled to the West of England Fat Stock and Poultry Exhibition. Galton was convinced (and spent much of his career up to this point seeking to prove) that only a small, select population had the necessary skills, training, expertise, intelligence, and other characteristics required to keep societies healthy. The average person, in Galton's professional opinion, contained so much "stupidity and wrong-headedness . . . as to be scarcely credible."[6]

To Galton, this fair seemed like the perfect opportunity to gather additional evidence for his theory. On that fated day in early twentieth-century England, visitors to the fair were invited to guess the weight of an ox. You may have had a chance at some point to win a prize by accurately guessing the number of jelly beans in a jar, or something similar. Galton surmised that "the average competitor was probably as well fitted for making a just estimate of the dressed weight of the ox, as an average voter is of judging the merits of most political issues on which he votes."[7] Regardless

---

6. Surowiecki, *Wisdom of Crowds*, xii.
7. Ibid.

of whether or not his comparative supposition was accurate, it was most certainly not accurate in the way he imagined!

After the competition, Galton took the nearly eight hundred submissions and discovered that while individual entries varied wildly, the average guess was pretty close. How close? The crowd's aggregate guess was 1,197 pounds.

The correct weight was 1,198 pounds.

This very diverse crowd, comprised mainly of people who would not much appreciate Galton's opinion of them, produced an answer that was remarkably close to perfect. The scientist found mind-boggling wisdom where he had anticipated mind-numbing ignorance.

To be sure, crowds often display great ignorance and countless other blunders. Who hasn't seen the effects of "mob mentality" and groupthink? Swayed by strong emotions, destabilizing events, or the influence of persuasive rhetoric, or all of these, crowds can be more than ignorant—they can be absolutely destructive.

Surowiecki suggests that there is indeed a hidden brilliance in diverse groups of individuals, but only under the right circumstances. His work suggests four key factors needed to tap into that wisdom:

1. *Diversity*: This includes opinions, perspectives, and experiences. The greater the diversity, the greater the possibility for collective wisdom. Homogeneity, particularly when it is expected, demanded, or rigidly enforced, tends to resist wisdom.

2. *Independence*: Wisdom flourishes in a crowd when people's opinions aren't determined by the opinions of those around them. You have seen this principle at work if you've noticed that a show-of-hands vote will typically produce a very different outcome than a secret ballot.

3. *Decentralization*: Wisdom flourishes when diverse, independent people are given the opportunity to specialize and draw on local knowledge. Wisdom languishes when the discussion

and decision-making is tightly contained, controlled, or narrowly defined.

4. *Aggregation*: It might seem too obvious to warrant mention, but the weight-guessing wisdom of the crowd at the fair would have still been present, but unrealized, if someone hadn't gathered, compiled, and compared the collective data.

In the beginning of this book we discussed Hunsberger's four streams of missional hermeneutic: (1) the missional direction of the story, (2) the missional purpose of the story, (3) the missional identity of the recipients, and (4) the missional engagement of culture.

Surowiecki and, perhaps to his chagrin, Galton have given us a clear example from social science as to why and how the missional identity and missional engagement streams are just as important as the direction and purpose of the story.

How much wisdom has been lost throughout the years as people handed the Bible (and the life of discipleship) to the "select, well-bred few?"[8] In fact, I suspect it is incredibly difficult to even recognize the missional direction and purpose of this story when it is interpreted, taught, and controlled by one person or one small subsection of the community.

This doesn't deny the valuable contribution of those who have dedicated their lives to theological and biblical studies. This isn't a rejection of clergy or seminary training any more than it is a rejection of the church.[9] This is not a zero-sum game; the goal is not to transfer control of the story from the one group to another. We will find neither justice nor benefit in rejecting or silencing those we believe have had too much control in the past—any more than we will find justice in continuing to ignore those who have not.

---

8. Ibid.

9. Addressing these same possible interpretations regarding the new monastic movement, Jonathan Wilson-Hartgrove says, "We're not trying to leave the church behind and do something new on our own. No, we are children of the church . . . We long for community because we've heard rumors of a new humanity . . . We are finding our way with Jesus, and what we're finding is that we need the Church" (*New Monasticism*, 141).

Little Children and One Fat Ox

After risking everything to get the Bible into the hands of "the common people," Martin Luther seemed to have a mixed reaction to the sixteenth-century German peasant revolt that came about as a direct result of his, and other reformers', efforts.

On the one hand, he openly supported the justness of the peasants' cause; yet he also lamented and publicly condemned the violent and disruptive behaviors associated with it. Some scholars and historians suggest that Luther's reactions "narrowed forevermore the original social promise of the Reformation."[10] The peasant revolt and Luther's subsequent response may have provided critics and those "on the fence" with ample evidence for why the populist movement should be kept in check.

I can't deny that Luther's reactions against the peasants often seemed ironically violent. In his delightful little treatise entitled, "Against the Robbing and Murdering Peasants," Luther penned this cheery admonition: "Let everyone who can smite, slay, and stab [the peasant], secretly and openly, remembering that nothing can be more poisonous, hurtful, or devilish than a rebel."[11] However, I'm not totally convinced that this irony was also inconsistent. Luther had some very particular beliefs about how Christians should conduct themselves in the public arena. From the very beginning it seems that his primary concern wasn't whether the peasants had a valid complaint, but rather how they would conduct themselves as they pursued justice.

Perhaps the true challenge for Luther was not that of consistency, but of compassion, or even simply understanding what these peasants had endured. When we take into account the long history of violence, oppression, inequity, and injustice, combined with the ruling class's continued and apparently unyielding approval of that same system, it is not difficult to imagine such a revolt coming to pass. In fact, it is actually more challenging to conceive how it could have been avoided.

Galton's ox experiment was still four hundred years in the future, so it is doubtful that Luther or anyone else would have

---

10. Ozment, *Age of Reform*, 273.
11. Quoted in ibid., 284.

considered these events in light of the wisdom of crowds, per se. However, with five centuries of hindsight, we can see that, while diversity was certainly present, this crowd was afforded no independence, denied access to positions of visibility and had, basically, no public voice, making decentralization of power impossible, and because no one was listening to their stories they had no hope of their collective wisdom being aggregated. These peasants were primed to become a mob.

Whether or not Luther's expectations of the peasants were realistic, there was another very good reason for Luther to oppose a revolt. He hinted at such when he said, "From the start I had two fears. If the peasants became lords, the devil would become abbott; if these tyrants became lords, the devil's dam would become abbess. Therefore, I wanted to do two things: quiet the peasants and instruct the lords."[12]

From Luther's perspective, a violent revolt was unlikely to bring about the desired change, regardless who won the day. Either scenario would likely lead to more division, not less. The potential wisdom found in a diverse community of independent, decentralized voices simply could not be realized through hostility. All that was happening would merely serve to shift (rather than dismantle) the dynamics of polarization. Instead of a diverse community, this open conflict would only decide which group would have power.

When we speak of reading the Bible with a missional church, we are most definitely not speaking of rejecting, ignoring, or revolting against the larger church, nor are we rejecting the value of clergy or biblical scholars. We are describing the astounding, and yes, sometimes mind-boggling, wisdom that emerges when we engage the text of Scripture as well as the context of our neighborhood together. We do not limit ourselves to the expert's monologue, nor do we have a desire to stir up the mob to oust the "old tyrants" to make room for the new.

As we read, we witness God's mission of reconciliation unfolding in our midst. We seek out and embrace the community's diversity. We watch, listen, and add our own voices expectantly,

12. Ibid., 287.

anticipating something unexpected and beautiful as we invite the Holy Spirit to speak through the diversity of the whole community, which includes all those physically present as well as those who have come before.

Throughout the teachings and writings of the Missional Wisdom Foundation it is common to hear references to community as a means of grace. That's only natural given our conviction that humankind is created in the image of God; the one revealed to us as a Community of Love, a God who demonstrates the essence of love and community by making space for others to exist, cooperate, and co-create.

How can we not listen to one another when we are created in the image of this God who hears the cries of the poor and has repeatedly come near? This invitation to read the Bible in community is an invitation to read—and live—as we were created.

Regardless of my particular gifts, on any given day my guess about the ox's weight may be way off. So long as I never look beyond my own isolated guess, I'm unlikely to see how my limited perspective might just be part of a larger tapestry . . . not to mention an unexpected and mind-boggling combined wisdom.

The call to read the Bible as a missional church is an invitation to look beyond my (or your) isolated guess. We listen in community, collectively looking for signs of God's missional purpose and direction, reminding one another of our shared missional identity, and spurring one another toward missional engagement within our own contexts. This way of reading the Bible leads to wisdom, discernment, and insight, as well as inspiring imagination, hope, healing, and reconciliation.

Notes from Denise

Are we brave enough? Can we trust that this intimate, creative God, in whose image and likeness we are made, trusts us to be part of co-creating this new heaven and new earth?

WHAT KIND OF GOD?

Can we trust that the gifts we bring to the table are as important to that co-creation as those of others who may be more highly educated or experienced than ourselves?

Can we embrace the diversity, independence, decentralization, and aggregation necessary for our communities to find their collective wisdom?

Can we dare to keep what is best in our Christian traditions and to reach further back to the Wisdom of God from before time?

Do we dare? Do we dare not?

Bibliography

Adams, Richard. *Watership Down: A Novel.* New York: Scribner, 1972.
Austin, B. J. "Lessons from Katrina." *KERA News.* http://keranews.org/post/lessons-katrina.
Benét, Stephen Vincent. *John Brown's Body.* 1st Elephant Paperback ed. 1928. Reprint, Chicago: Ivan R. Dee, 1990.
Birch, Bruce, et al. *A Theological Introduction to the Old Testament.* Nashville: Abingdon, 1999.
Brueggemann, Walter. *Isaiah.* 2 vols. Westminster Bible Companion. Louisville: Westminster John Knox, 1998.
Chesterton, G. K. *On Chasing After One's Hat and Other Whimsies.* New York: Robert M. McBride, 1933.
Claiborne, Shane, Jonathan Wilson-Hartgrove, and Enuma Okoro. *Common Prayer: A Liturgy for Ordinary Radicals.* Grand Rapids: Zondervan, 2010.
Clark-Soles, Jaime. *Reading John for Dear Life: A Spiritual Walk with the Fourth Gospel.* Louisville: Westminster John Knox, 2016.
Collins, Courtney. "How North Texas Sheltered 26,000 Katrina Evacuees with No Disaster Plan." *KERA News,* August 28, 2015. http://keranews.org/post/how-north-texas-sheltered-26000-katrina-evacuees-no-disaster-plan.
deSilva, David A. *Honor, Patronage, Kinship and Purity: Unlocking New Testament Culture.* Downers Grove, IL: InterVarsity, 2000.
Duggins, Larry. *Simple Harmony: Thoughts on Holistic Christian Life.* CreateSpace, 2012.
―――. *Together: Community as a Means of Grace.* Eugene, OR: Cascade, 2017.
Fee, Gordon D., and Douglas Stuart. *How to Read the Bible Book by Book: A Guided Tour.* Grand Rapids: Zondervan, 2002.
―――. *How to Read the Bible for All Its Worth.* 4th ed. Grand Rapids: Zondervan, 2014.
Fernandez, Manny, Richard Pérez-Peña, and Jonah Engel Bromwich. "Five Dallas Officers Were Killed as Payback, Police Chief Says." *New York Times,* July 8, 2016. http://www.nytimes.com/2016/07/09/us/dallas-police-shooting.html.

Bibliography

Flood, Derek. *Disarming Scripture: Cherry-Picking Liberals, Violence-Loving Conservatives, and Why We All Need to Learn to Read the Bible Like Jesus Did*. San Francisco: Metanoia, 2014.

Foster, Douglas A, et al., eds. *The Encyclopedia of the Stone-Campbell Movement*. Grand Rapids: Eerdmans, 2004.

Frankl, Victor. *Man's Search for Meaning*. New York: Washington Square, 1984.

Heath, Elaine A., ed. *Abide: A Guide to Living in Intentional Community*. Missional Wisdom Foundation, 2014.

———. *Naked Faith: The Mystical Theology of Phoebe Palmer*. Eugene, OR: Pickwick, 2009.

Hirsch, Alan N., and David W. Ferguson. *On the Verge: A Journey into the Apostolic Future of the Church*. Grand Rapids: Zondervan, 2011.

Hughes, Richard T. *Reviving the Ancient Faith: The Story of Churches of Christ in America*. Grand Rapids: Eerdmans, 1996.

Hunsberger, George R. "Proposals for a Missional Hermeneutic: Mapping a Conversation." *Missiology: An International Review* 39 (2011) 309–21.

Koester, Craig R. *Revelation and the End of All Things*. Grand Rapids: Eerdmans, 2001.

Lincoln, Abraham. "The Gettysburg Address." *Abraham Lincoln Online*. https://www.abrahamlincolnonline.org/lincoln/speeches/gettysburg.html.

McLaren, Brian. *The Secret Message of Jesus: Uncovering the Truth That Could Change Everything*. Nashville: W Publishing Group, 2006.

Ozment, Steven. *The Age of Reform, 1250–1550: An Intellectual and Religious History of Late Medieval and Reformation Europe*. New Haven: Yale University Press, 1980.

Pearle, Lauren. "School Shootings since Columbine: By the Numbers." *ABC News*, February 12, 2016. http://abcnews.go.com/US/school-shootings-columbine-numbers/story?id=36833245.

Reid, Daniel G., ed. *The IVP Dictionary of the New Testament: A One-Volume Compendium of Contemporary Biblical Scholarship*. Downers Grove, IL: InterVarsity, 2004.

Roxburgh, Alan J., and Fred Romanuk. *The Missional Leader: Equipping Your Church to Reach a Changing World*. San Francisco: Jossey-Bass, 2006.

Surowiecki, James. *The Wisdom of Crowds*. New York: Anchor, 2005.

Taylor, Daniel. *Tell Me a Story: The Life-Shaping Power of Our Stories*. St. Paul, MN: Bog Walk, 1996.

Volf, Miroslav. "The Redemption of Touch." Sermon delivered at First Presbyterian Church, Durham, North Carolina, February 26, 2017.

Wilson-Hartgrove, Jonathan. *The New Monasticism: What It Has to Say to Today's Church*. Grand Rapids: Baker, 2008.

———. *The Wisdom of Stability: Rooting Faith in a Mobile Culture*. Brewster, MA: Paraclete, 2010.

Wright, Christopher J. H. *The Mission of God: Unlocking the Bible's Grand Narrative*. Downers Grove, IL: InterVarsity, 2006.

———. *The Mission of God's People: A Biblical Theology of the Church's Mission.* Biblical Theology for Life. Grand Rapids: Zondervan, 2010.

www.ingramcontent.com/pod-product-compliance
Lightning Source LLC
Chambersburg PA
CBHW032156160426
43197CB00008B/942